5-MINUTE RETIREMENT DEVOTIONALS FOR WOMEN

Simple Daily Faith Journey to Rediscover Purpose, Peace, and Create Meaning After Retirement

© Copyright 2025. JA Sterling. All rights reserved.

The content contained within this book may not be reproduced, duplicated, or transmitted without direct written permission from the author or the publisher.

Under no circumstances will any blame or legal responsibility be held against the publisher or author for any damages, reparation, or monetary loss due to the information contained within this book, either directly or indirectly.

Legal Notice

This book is copyright-protected. It is only for personal use. You cannot amend, distribute, sell, use, quote, or paraphrase any part of this book's content without the author's or publisher's consent.

Disclaimer Notice

Please note that the information contained within this document is for educational and entertainment purposes only. All efforts have been executed to present accurate, up-to-date, reliable, and complete information. No warranties of any kind are declared or implied. Readers acknowledge that the author does not render legal, financial, medical, or professional advice. The content within this book has been derived from various sources. Please consult a licensed professional before attempting any techniques outlined in this book.

By reading this document, the reader agrees that under no circumstances is the author responsible for any direct or indirect losses incurred due to the use of the information contained within this document, including, but not limited to, errors, omissions, or inaccuracies.

JA STERLING

TABLE OF CONTENTS

A Letter from the Matriarch

The Call to Refinement

Welcome to the Third Act. If you are holding this book, it is likely because the quiet of your home has begun to speak louder than the noise of your former office. You have spent decades as a professional: a woman of competence, a navigator of complex systems, and a pillar of your community. For years, your identity was forged in the heat of "doing." You were defined by the titles on your business cards, the deadlines on your calendar, and the persistent needs of the people who relied on your expertise.

Then, the final commute ended.

The transition into retirement is often marketed to women as a sunny, permanent vacation: a season of endless leisure and watercolor sunsets. However, for the professional Christian woman, this transition is   rarely that simple. It is often an ontological crisis, a fundamental shaking of the self that occurs when the "worker" is stripped away to reveal the "being" underneath. You may find yourself staring at the "void" of unstructured time with a sense of dread rather than delight. You may feel unmoored, invisible, or even spiritually stagnant.

This is not a failure of faith; it is a call to a deeper theology.

For too long, the resources provided to women in this season have been what I call "pink fluff." They offer emotional platitudes and shallow comfort, treating the retired woman as if her intellectual capacity has diminished along with her professional obligations. I reject this notion. You do not need a "watered-down latte" of a devotional; you need a "shot of espresso." You need a faith that is robust enough to handle the hard questions of family estrangement, grandmother burnout, and the deconstruction of long-held dogmas.

This book is designed to be your "Authenticity Compass." It is a 52-week liturgy intended to help you move from a "work-driven" life to a "legacy-driven" calling. We will not shy away from the negative space of retirement. We will lean into the Greek and Hebrew origins of our faith to find the intellectual anchors your soul requires. We will learn to celebrate "Refirement": the process of letting the Holy Spirit refine the wisdom of your years into a potent force for the Kingdom.

You are not becoming irrelevant. You are becoming a Matriarch. The church and your family do not need your labor as much as they need your wisdom, your prayer, and your consecrated presence. It is time to stop "doing" for a moment and learn the sacred art of "being."

May these pages serve as a stabilizing anchor in your daily rhythm. May they challenge your mind and comfort your spirit as you navigate this wilderness. Welcome to the season where you finally have the time to become exactly who God always intended you to be.

The Liturgy of the Third Act

How to Use This Book

This is not a book to be rushed. It is designed to fit into a five-minute daily window, providing a high-substance spiritual snack that sets the tone for your entire day. Because you are a woman of discipline, we have structured each week around a "Liturgy of the Third Act."

Each week is presented as a two-page spread. The left page provides the theological depth, while the right page provides the space for your personal refinement and active response.

The Six Components of Your Weekly Rhythms:

1. The Biblical Standard (The Morning Anchor)

Every week begins with a full scripture passage from the New Living Translation (NLT). We have printed the text in its entirety to ensure you can stay in the "flow" of your five-minute window without the friction of looking up references. This is your Morning Anchor: the first word spoken over your day.

2. The Word Study (The Commute to the Throne)

Immediately following the scripture, you will find a specific Greek or Hebrew word study. These are included to respect your intellectual capacity and to provide a deeper, more rigorous understanding of the biblical text. We will explore the linguistic roots of terms like Shabbat, poiema, and Chochmah, ensuring that your devotional time remains educationally stimulating.

3. The Theological Reflection (The Noon Anchor)

The core of the left page is a 250- to 300-word reflection. These are dense, logical, and theological essays that avoid surface-level fluff. They are designed to be your Noon Anchor, a moment to recenter your mind when the day feels driftless or the "void" of retirement begins to feel heavy.

4. Matriarch's Reflection Questions

On the right page, you will find three targeted questions designed to challenge your thinking and apply the theology of the week to your specific life stage. These are not general inquiries, but architectural tools for the soul.

5. Next Step Action Items

Meaning-making requires action. We provide two specific, manageable "Faith-in-Action" microchallenges each week. These ensure that your spiritual growth is translated into tangible changes in your boundaries, your schedule, and your relationships.

6. Prayer and Refining Space

Each week concludes with a direct prayer to the Father, centering the week's theme in a posture of surrender. Below this is the "Refining Space": a generous ruled section for your own journaling. Use this space to respond to the Matriarch Prompts provided.

By following this simple, daily rhythm, you are creating a new "Rule of Life" for your retirement. You are replacing the structure of the 9-to-5 with the superior structure of a life lived in intentional presence. Let us begin.

01

<hr>

THE ONTOLOGICAL
DECONSTRUCTION

<hr>

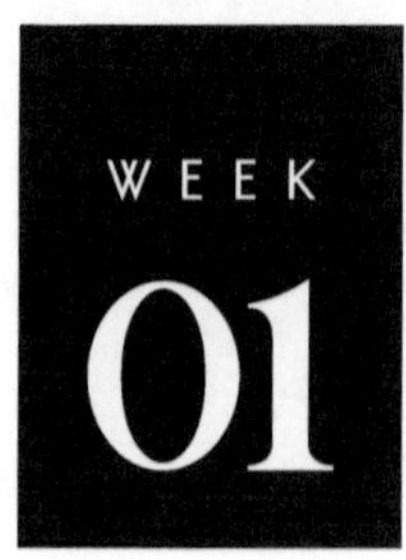

WEEK 01

THE FINAL COMMUTE

> Then Jesus said, 'Come to me, all of you who are weary and carry heavy burdens, and I will give you rest. Take my yoke upon you. Let me teach you, because I am humble and gentle at heart, and you will find rest for your souls.
>
> — *Matthew 11:28-29 (NLT)*

 **The Morning Anchor**

The Greek word *anapausis* means a restorative cessation from labor, bringing a new beginning. For the professional woman, it is the holy intermission between your career's "doing" and your legacy's "being", a purposeful pause recalibrating your soul toward the Creator.

 **The Noon Anchor**

For decades, your identity synchronized with your commute—a daily ritual of putting on professional armor. Now, that vanished routine leaves a silence that can feel like grieving lost status.

This profound vertigo reveals how deeply we idolize the "worker" identity, linking our immense worth to our output. Yet, Jesus gently invites you to deconstruct the exhausting belief that you must earn your right to exist. He calls you not to find strength for more labor, but to discover the beautiful, restful humility of simply being His.

Reflection Questions

01   When you are asked "What do you do?", what is the first feeling that rises in your chest, and why?

02   How much of your self-worth relies on professional competence rather than spiritual identity?

03   What was the "armor" you put on during your commute, and why does it feel so difficult to lay it down?

Next Steps

☐   **The Status Surrender:** Identify one physical symbol of your former career (a badge, a nameplate, a specific professional bag) and consciously pray over it, surrendering your status to God.

☐   **The Reflex Audit:** Spend this week observing how often you reflexively check your professional emails or calendar, and replace each urge with the word anapausis.

Heavenly Father, I confess that I have carried the heavy burdens of my career for too long. I am weary from the effort of maintaining my own status. Today, I accept Your invitation to find rest. Teach me to be humble and gentle at heart. Let me find my identity in Your calling rather than my former commute. Amen.

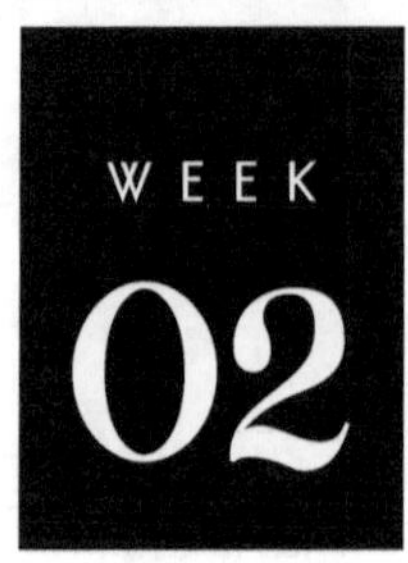

WEEK 02

SHABBAT: THE COMMAND TO CEASE

> On the seventh day God had finished his work of creation, so he rested from all his work. And God blessed the seventh day and declared it holy, because it was the day when he rested from all his work of creation.
>
> — *Genesis 2:2-3 (NLT)*

The Morning Anchor

The Hebrew word *Shabbat* beautifully means "to cease." It is not about recovering from fatigue, but celebrating completion, like a king taking residence in his temple. Sabbath declares that the world is sustained by God's power, not our endless effort.

The Noon Anchor

The greatest hurdle for the retired professional is the internal drive that refuses to cease. After decades of sustaining systems, this sudden rest can falsely feel like a lazy spiritual failure. Yet, Shabbat is a holy command.

Humanity's very first full day was a day of rest, revealing we are beautifully created to begin from a place of "finishedness," not striving. Retirement is your massive, extended *Shabbat*—a divine invitation to inhabit your life's temple, surrendering outcomes to God, and learning the holy art of stopping.

Reflection Questions

01 Why does "stopping" feel like a threat to your sense of self rather than a holy invitation?

02 In what areas are you still acting as a "sustainer of systems" as if God cannot rule without you?

03 How would your week change if you truly believed that your work was "finished" in the eyes of the Father?

Next Steps

☐ **The Holy Hour of Nothing:** Choose one hour this week to do absolutely nothing "productive." No laundry, no errands, no organizing. Simply practice being present.

☐ **The Guilt Filter:** Every time you feel guilty for being still, speak the word Shabbat out loud as a reminder of God's command to cease.

Heavenly Father, I thank You that the world is sustained by Your hand and not my effort. Forgive me for my frantic striving and my fear of stopping. I choose to inhabit this season of Shabbat. Teach me to celebrate the work You have finished in me and to trust Your rule over my life. Amen.

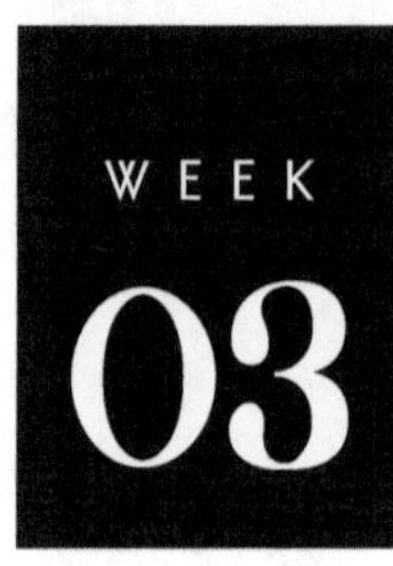

03

IDENTITY WITHOUT THE TITLE

> See how very much our Father loves us, for he calls us his children, and that is what we are! But the people who belong to this world don't recognize that we are God's children because they don't know him.
>
> — *1 John 3:1 (NLT)*

 **The Morning Anchor**

The Greek word *teknon* signifies a child born of a parent, emphasizing a shared spiritual nature. Unlike professional titles you earn, this is a permanent, inherited status from your Father's house—a foundational identity existing beautifully before any degree or promotion.

 **The Noon Anchor**

Losing professional titles can feel like a social death, tempting you to scramble for new labels. Yet, relevance is a worldly metric. The Father sees only the teknon, your true identity given at baptism, long before any career.

The world cannot fathom value that is not produced. When earthly recognition fades, do not despair. It is a beautiful sign that you are moving deeper into the profound reality of God's house.

Reflection Questions

01 Which professional title was the hardest for you to lose, and what "burden" did it force you to carry?

02 Are you currently trying to "collect" new volunteer or social titles to replace the identity you lost?

03 How does being a teknon change how you enter a room where no one knows your credentials?

Next Steps

☐ **The Title-Free Introduction:** The next time someone asks "What do you do?", answer by describing what you are learning about God rather than using your former title.

☐ **The Inheritance List:** Write down three things you have "inherited" as a child of God that no job title could ever provide.

Heavenly Father, I thank You that I am Your child, born of Your Spirit. Forgive me for seeking the recognition of the world and the security of my titles. I rest in the dignity of my inheritance as Your teknon. Help me to find my worth in Your love alone. Amen.

A FREE GIFT TO OUR READERS

BONUS

When you lost your business card, did
you lose your soul?

THE IDENTITY DECONSTRUCTION AUDIT

Inside, you'll find...

- Guides you in stripping away the "worker bee" persona to find the Poiema (God's masterpiece) underneath.
- Delivers a rigorous workbook focusing on the theological concept of Kenosis, or self-emptying.
- Features ten "Identity-Free" reflection questions and a detailed "Title vs. Calling" comparison chart.

And more!

Download your FREE BONUS now!

https://mentalgrowthpublishing.com/retirement-devotional

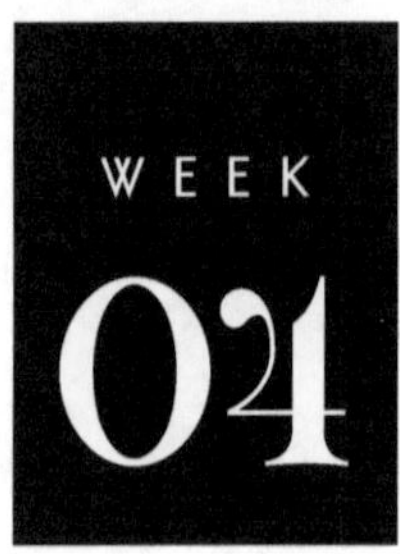

04

THEOLOGY OF THE VOID

> The earth was formless and empty, and darkness covered the deep waters. And the Spirit of God was hovering over the surface of the waters.
>
> — *Genesis 1:2 (NLT)*

The Morning Anchor

The Hebrew phrase tohu wa-bohu translates to a formless, profound emptiness. Yet, in the grand biblical narrative, this desolate wasteland is never the end of the story. Instead, it serves as the raw material for divine creation. It is the essential void where God's Spirit patiently hovers before a beautiful, entirely new thing finally emerges.

The Noon Anchor

Retirement's initial thrill often yields to a stark, unstructured void. Terrified of this silence, many rush to fill the emptiness with frantic busyness, mistaking stillness for stagnation. Yet, God's Spirit does His most beautiful work in the tohu wa-bohu.

This vast vacuum is not an absence of purpose, but a profound presence of potential—the sacred monastic cell of your Third Act. Here, God creates space for a new calling. Embrace the quiet to ask: Who am I without tasks, and is God enough when I am not useful?

Reflection Questions

01 When you look at an empty calendar, do you feel a sense of peace or a sense of panic?

02 What "quiet questions" have you been avoiding by filling your time with busy distractions?

03 How can you transform the "wasteland" of your unstructured time into a "raw material" for God's Spirit?

Next Steps

☐ **The Calendar Cleanse:** Identify one upcoming obligation that you only added to "feel busy" and remove it.

☐ **The Hovering Practice:** Spend fifteen minutes in complete silence each day this week, inviting the Holy Spirit to "hover" over the empty spaces in your soul.

Heavenly Father, I admit that the emptiness of this season frightens me. Forgive me for trying to fill the void with noise and busyness. I choose to trust that Your Spirit is hovering over my life. Use this tohu wa-bohu to create something new in me. Let me find peace in the potential of Your presence. Amen.

PERMISSION TO REST

> It is useless for you to work so hard from early morning until late at night, toiling for food to eat! For God gives rest to his loved ones.
>
> — *Psalm 127:2 (NLT)*

The Morning Anchor 

The Hebrew word *shenah* signifies a deep, peaceful security offering true physical and mental rest. As the beautiful antithesis of anxious toil, shenah is never a reward for exhausted effort. It is a divine grace lovingly bestowed upon God's beloved.

The Noon Anchor

For decades, you equated endless toil with faithfulness, believing your security depended on your effort. Now, without your career's structure, resting may feel like a moral failure, sparking frantic busyness to avoid the vulnerability of stillness. Yet, anxious toiling is functional atheism—believing the world stops if you do.

Retirement beautifully tests your trust in God as Provider. If resting brings guilt, productivity has become an idol. God lovingly gives shenah to remind you that your profound significance is sustained by His hand alone, not your exhaustion.

01 What specific fear rises in you when you are not actively "producing" something?

02 How has "anxious toil" prevented you from receiving the gift of deep security in God?

03 In what ways are you trying to earn your right to exist through your ongoing labor in retirement?

Next Steps

☐ **The Guilt-Driven Cancelation:** Identify one task this week that you are doing only to feel "useful" and cancel it. Spend that time in intentional rest.

☐ **The Shenah Prayer:** Each night before you sleep, specifically name one worry you are handing over to the Provider, accepting His gift of rest.

Heavenly Father, I confess that I have often believed my security was the result of my own toil. Forgive me for making an idol of my hard work. I accept Your permission to rest today. Teach me to trust that You are my Provider and that my significance is found in Being Your loved one. Amen.

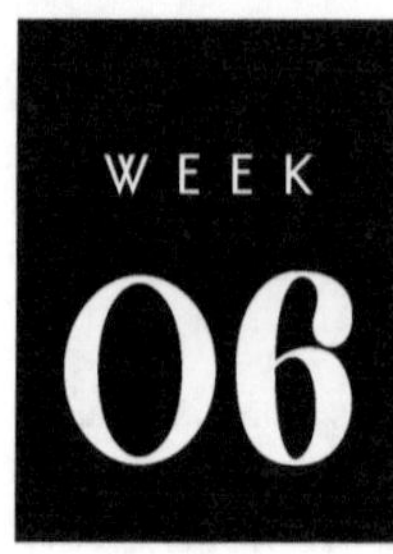

KENOSIS: THE EMPTYING

> You must have the same attitude that Christ Jesus had. Though he was God, he did not think of equality with God as something to cling to. Instead, he gave up his divine privileges; he took the humble position of a slave and was born as a human being.
>
> — *Philippians 2:5-7 (NLT)*

The Morning Anchor

The Greek word *kenosis* signifies voluntarily pouring out status for a higher purpose, just as Christ emptied Himself. For the retiree, this means releasing professional ego to embrace a humble mission. It is the beautiful transition from authority to servant.

The Noon Anchor

Your professional life demanded clinging to authority, yet carrying that spirit into retirement often breeds bitterness. The Third Act calls for kenosis—the voluntary emptying of former privileges. This is not a diminishment of worth, but a sacred imitation of your Savior. By laying down the heavy garment of professional ego, you finally free your hands to receive who you are becoming.

Cease clinging to the past to fully embrace your beautiful, humble role as a spiritual mother.

Reflection Questions

01   What "divine privilege" of your former career are you still trying to cling to in your retirement?

02   How does the urge to "be the authority" prevent you from inhabiting the humble mission of a servant?

03   Where in your life is your professional ego acting as a barrier to new spiritual growth?

Next Steps

☐ **The Silent Observation:** Attend a meeting or gathering this week and consciously choose to listen more than you speak. Resist the urge to assert your expertise.

☐ **The Ego Pour:** Identify one title or reputation you once enjoyed and visualize yourself "pouring it out" as a gift to God, asking Him to fill that space with His Spirit.

Heavenly Father, I thank You for the example of Christ, who emptied Himself for my sake. Forgive me for clinging to my status and my need for authority. I choose to lay down my professional ego today. Empty me of my pride so that I may be filled with Your humble purpose. Amen.

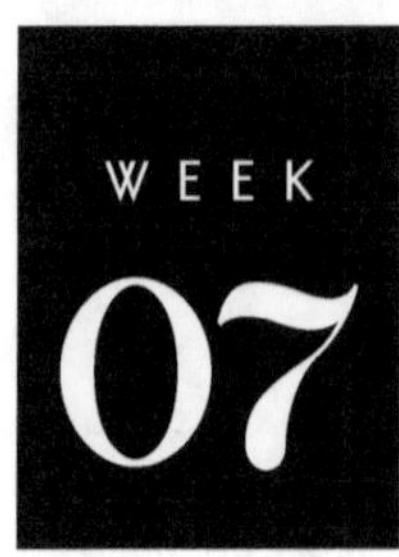

THE LAST FIRST DAY

> So don't worry about these things, saying, 'What will we eat? What will we drink? What will we wear?' These things dominate the thoughts of unbelievers, but your heavenly Father already knows all your needs. Seek the Kingdom of God above all else, and live righteously, and he will give you everything you need.
>
> — *Matthew 6:31-33 (NLT)*

 **The Morning Anchor**

The Greek word *zeteo* means a persistent, deliberate search for immense value. It is not casual looking, but a sacred craving. To zeteo is to beautifully redirect your earthly ambition, making the eternal Kingdom of God your soul's devoted calling.

 **The Noon Anchor**

When retirement's initial honeymoon gently fades, the comforting rhythm of familiar deadlines and earthly striving dissolves, often sparking a quiet anxiety. Accustomed to chasing promotions or daily provisions, it is deeply tempting to drift into passive leisure, quietly abandoning your spiritual vitality. Yet, as a wise Matriarch, you are called to a vastly higher, beautiful pursuit. This sacred season is your divine opportunity to finally *zeteo* the Kingdom of God. Lovingly redirect your profound earthly discipline toward the glorious pursuit of His eternal righteousness.

Reflection Questions

01 How has the end of your "professional ambition" caused a hidden sense of anxiety in your soul?

02 Are you currently "quiet quitting" your spiritual life by seeking leisure over the Kingdom?

03 What would it look like to apply the same discipline from your career to your search for God's righteousness?

Next Steps

☐ **The Ambition Audit:** Look at your search history or your reading list this week. Are you seeking entertainment more than you are seeking the Kingdom? Redraw your focus.

☐ **The Zeteo Hour:** Dedicate one hour each day this week to the concentrated search for God's Kingdom through prayer, study, or service.

Heavenly Father, I confess that my thoughts are often dominated by my worries and my search for worldly security. Forgive me for my lack of spiritual ambition. Today, I choose to seek Your Kingdom above all else. Redirect my discipline and my craving toward Your righteousness. Amen.

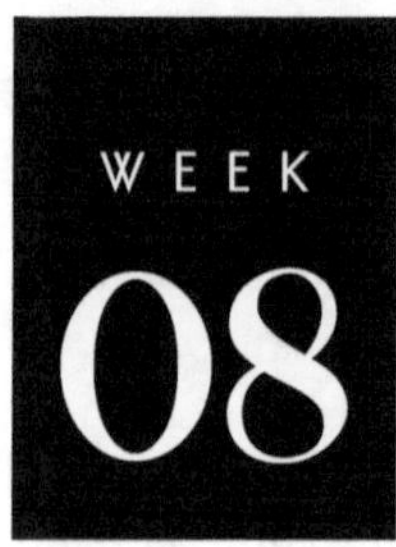

NUMBERING OUR DAYS

Teach us to realize the brevity of life, so that we may grow in wisdom.

— Psalm 90:12 (NLT)

The Morning Anchor

The Hebrew word *manah* means to weigh with care, like measuring precious silver. To manah your days is to treat time as a sacred currency—not merely spent, but intentionally invested. This mindful numbering is the beautiful foundation of spiritual stewardship.

The Noon Anchor

In your career, you mastered managing time for earthly organizations. In this beautiful "Third Act," the rhythm shifts: you are numbering days for your soul. Yet, boundless time can easily drift into trivial distraction. The psalmist gently calls us to embrace our finitude with grace.

By choosing to manah your days, you realize these golden years are a sacred capstone to consecrate, not a bonus to squander. Every quiet afternoon is precious silver placed in your hand by the Creator. How will you lovingly steward the divine currency of your remaining years?

01 How much of your current weekly schedule is spent on "spending" time versus "investing" it in eternal things?

02 What specific "silver coins" of your time are you squandering on digital distractions or trivialities?

03 How does the reality of the brevity of life change your perspective on your "fruitfulness" this month?

Next Steps

☐ **The Time Budget:** Track your time for one full day this week. Identify where you are "drifting" and consciously "appoint" that time to a godly purpose.

☐ **The Wisdom Investment:** Choose one activity this week that has no "productive" value but deep "wisdom" value, such as a long conversation with an old friend or a deep study of a Psalm.

Heavenly Father, I thank You for the gift of these days. Forgive me for squandering the precious currency of my time on things that do not last. Teach me to number my days with care. Grant me the wisdom to invest my life in Your eternal Kingdom so that I may be fruitful in my later years. Amen.

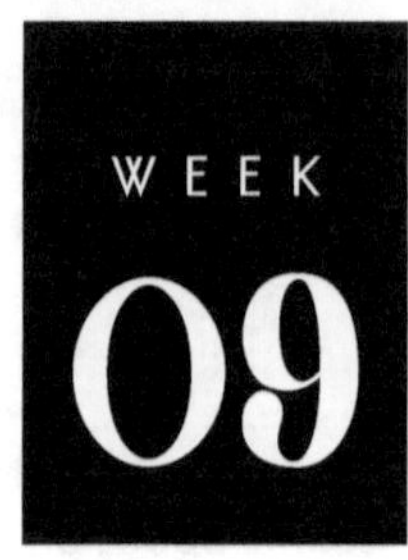

THE IDOL OF PRODUCTIVITY

> *God saved you by his grace when you believed. And you can't take credit for this; it is a gift from God. Salvation is not a reward for the good things we have done, so none of us can boast about it. For we are God's masterpiece. He has created us anew in Christ Jesus, so we can do the good things he planned for us long ago.*
>
> — *Ephesians 2:8-10 (NLT)*

 **The Morning Anchor**

The Greek word *poiema* translates to "masterpiece" or "poem," signifying a work carefully crafted by a master artisan. Your immense value is not found in what you produce, but in being God's beautiful art before you ever perform a task.

 **The Noon Anchor**

For years, your peace was tied to conquering demanding to-do lists. In retirement, an empty schedule can spark panic, tempting you to manufacture busywork to feel secure. Yet, this restless drive is an idol. The Gospel beautifully declares you are God's *poiema*. A masterpiece does not strive to justify its existence; its profound value rests in the Creator's signature. God gently invites you to cease striving, rest in His holy craftsmanship, and let His planned good works naturally flow from a soul renewed in Christ.

Reflection Questions

01 If your ability to "produce" was permanently taken away, what would be the primary source of your dignity?

02 In what specific ways have you used "busyness" as a shield to avoid the quiet presence of God?

03 How does the imagery of being a "poem" change your perspective on a day that feels unproductive?

Next Steps

☐ **The "Did-Be" Audit:** At the end of each day, write down three moments where you simply "were" a child of God rather than a worker.

☐ **The List Fast:** Go one full day without writing or checking a to-do list. Observe the physical sensations of anxiety that arise and meet them with the word poiema.

Heavenly Father, I confess that I have often worshipped the work of my own hands. I have used my productivity to hide my insecurity. Today, I surrender my lists and my need for utility. Teach me to sit in the stillness as Your poiema. Let me find my dignity in Your signature alone. I trust that Your grace is sufficient for my empty hours. Amen.

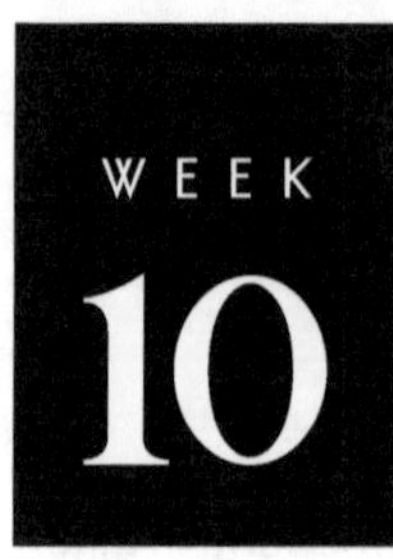

INTELLECTUAL HUNGER

> *Don't copy the behavior and customs of this world, but let God transform you into a new person by changing the way you think. Then you will learn to know God's will for you, which is good and pleasing and perfect.*
>
> — *Romans 12:2 (NLT)*

The Morning Anchor

The Greek word *anakainosis* means a complete, beautiful renovation of the mind. It is a fundamental restructuring of your intellect to align with God's eternal truth. This gracefully shifts your rigorous professional development into a passionate, intentional theological pursuit.

The Noon Anchor

Retirement often brings an unspoken struggle: the sudden quiet of a highly capable, intellectually starved mind. While the world expects you to embrace trivial leisure, your soul craves profound substance. This mental restlessness is a divine invitation. For decades, your brilliant intellect was rented by earthly obligations; now, it is fully yours to consecrate. This is your sacred season for *anakainosis*. Lovingly redirect your professional rigor to study His depths, becoming a radiant theologian in residence. God desires to beautifully renovate your mind, not merely quiet it.

Reflection Questions

01 What was the last "difficult" theological concept you wrestled with, and how did it change your view of God?

02 Are you settling for spiritual "milk" because you think your intellectual peak is behind you?

03 How can you use your professional expertise to help younger believers navigate the challenges of faith?

Next Steps

☐ **The Theological Syllabus:** Select one book of the Bible and one reputable academic commentary. Commit to thirty minutes of "deep study" each day this week.

☐ **The Custom Challenge:** Identify one "custom of this world" that has influenced your thinking lately and research the biblical counter-argument.

Heavenly Father, I thank You for the capacity of the mind You have given me. Forgive me for settling for shallow waters when You have called me to the deep. I dedicate my intellect to Your service. Renovate my thinking through Your Word. Let my hunger lead me to a more perfect knowledge of Your will. Grant me the discipline to seek You with all my strength. Amen.

A FREE GIFT TO OUR READERS

BONUS

You do not want fluff; you want the
original Word.

THE
MATRIARCH'S LEXICON
A Hebrew & Greek
Cheat Sheet

Inside, you'll find...

- Serves as a professional-grade reference guide for the 52 key terms used throughout the book.
- Catalogs every Greek and Hebrew word from the curriculum alongside its phonetic spelling.
- Delivers original meanings and one-sentence theological definitions to strengthen your deep daily study.

And more!

Download your FREE BONUS now!

https://mentalgrowthpublishing.com/retirement-devotional

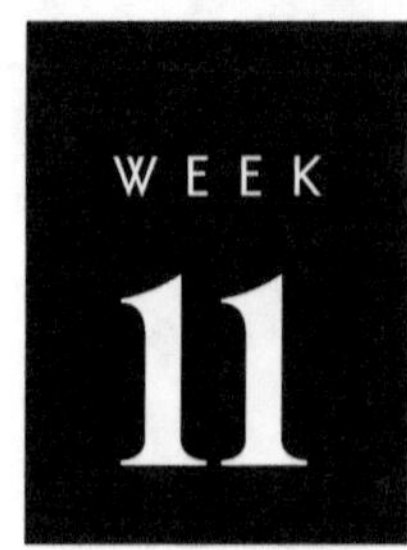

11

THE RULE OF LIFE

> This is what the Lord says: 'Stop at the crossroads and look around. Ask for the old, godly way, and walk in it. Travel its path, and you will find rest for your souls.
>
> — *Jeremiah 6:16 (NLT)*

The Morning Anchor

The Hebrew word *netibah* signifies an established path or a "Rule of Life." Like a sturdy trellis supporting a growing vine, these sacred habits provide vital spiritual structure, protecting your soul from collapsing under the weight of newfound freedom.

The Noon Anchor

Retirement opens to a vast crossroads. Without the familiar 9-to-5 *netibah*, this sudden lack of structure can cause dangerous spiritual drift, trading true rest for restlessness amid digital noise.

To flourish, your soul requires a beautifully intentional "Rule of Life." This is not legalism, but a sacred trellis of chosen habits—a daily rhythm of prayer, study, and gentle service replacing your professional calendar. You are no longer a slave to earthly urgency, but a radiant steward of this new season's divine importance.

01 Does your current daily schedule reflect your highest values or merely your loudest interruptions?

02 If you were to design a "trellis" for your soul, what three habits would be the most stabilizing?

03 Where in your day do you feel the most "drift," and what ritual could you implement to anchor yourself?

Next Steps

The Anchor Map: Designate three "anchors" for your day: a specific time for the Morning Anchor, the Noon Anchor, and the Evening Examen. Set alarms on your phone to remind you of these holy appointments.

The Digital Boundary: Set a "start" and "stop" time for all digital devices to prevent them from encroaching on your netibah.

Heavenly Father, I stand at the crossroads of this new season and I look to You. Forgive my aimless wandering and my lack of holy rhythm. Help me to build a trellis of godly habits that will sustain my soul. I choose to walk the ancient path of prayer and presence. Structure my days by Your Spirit so that I may find true rest in You. Amen.

A FREE GIFT TO OUR READERS

BONUS

Without a schedule, the "Void" will
swallow your days.

THE "RULE OF LIFE" PLANNER PAGE

Inside, you'll find...

- Assists you in building a "Monastery of the Home" with a daily rhythm that strictly prioritizes the soul.
- Transforms your daily planning by replacing frantic "To-Do" lists with stabilizing "To-Be" anchors.
- Structures your day with dedicated sections for the Morning Commute to the Throne, the Noon Anchor, and the Evening Examen.

And more!

Download your FREE BONUS now!

https://mentalgrowthpublishing.com/retirement-devotional

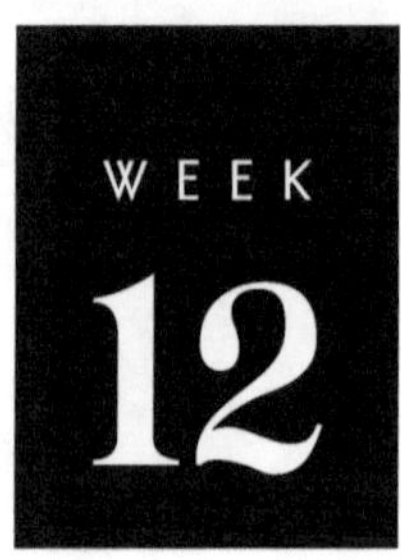

12

GRAY HAIR AS A CROWN

> Gray hair is a crown of glory; it is gained by living a godly life.
>
> — *Proverbs 16:31 (NLT)*

The Morning Anchor

The Hebrew word *tipharah* signifies radiant glory, like the high priest's majestic garments. Gray hair is not a sign of fading invisibility, but a beautiful, visible crown of faithfulness. It is the sacred uniform of the Matriarch, radiating profound authority and wisdom.

The Noon Anchor

Society often treats aging as a cruel fading into silent invisibility, unjustly stripping away the profound professional stature you held in your demanding career. This damaging cultural illusion can spark a deep spiritual crisis, constantly tempting you to frantically chase fleeting youth while your soul quietly starves for wisdom's true recognition. Yet, we must beautifully reclaim the biblical theology of *tipharah*. Your silver strands are not tragic marks of decline, but rather a sacred, gleaming crown of glory, testifying to hard battles won and enduring grace received. You are absolutely not fading; you are a magnificent Kingdom Matriarch, purposefully carrying the indispensable, hard-earned wisdom the modern church desperately needs today.

Reflection Questions

01 How much of your self-worth is still tied to the cultural standard of youth and visibility?

02 What specific battle or season in your life earned you a "silver strand" of wisdom?

03 How can you mentor a younger woman this week by sharing the "weight" of your *tipharah*?

Next Steps

☐ **The Mirror Declaration:** Look in the mirror and specifically name one trait of wisdom you have gained through aging. Declare it as a "crown of glory."

☐ **The Intentional Presence:** Attend a community gathering and consciously sit in a place of visibility. Speak a word of encouragement to a younger person from your place of authority.

Heavenly Father, I thank You for the crown You have placed upon my head. Forgive me for shrinking back in the face of cultural lies. I choose to wear my years with dignity and my silver with pride. Let my wisdom be a weight of glory in my community. Use my voice to speak Your truth into the next generation. I am Your splendor. Amen.

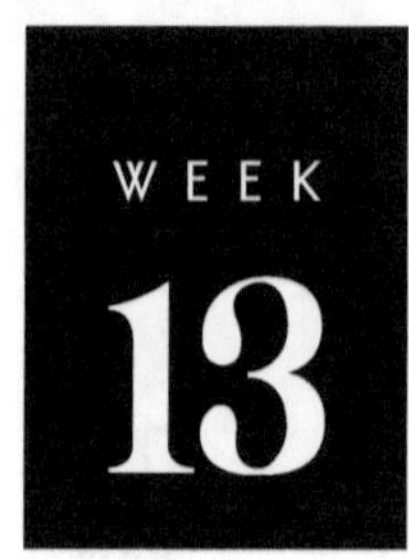

THE FIRST QUARTER REVIEW

> Samuel then took a large stone and placed it between the towns of Mizpah and Jeshanah. He named it Ebenezer (which means 'the stone of help'), for he said, 'Up to this point the Lord has helped us!
>
> — *1 Samuel 7:12 (NLT)*

 **The Morning Anchor** 

The Hebrew phrase *Eben-ha-ezer* means "Stone of the Help"—a sacred landmark commemorating divine victory. For the retiree, erecting an Ebenezer is a beautiful pause to reflect, declaring that "up to this point," the Lord has faithfully sustained your transition.

 **The Noon Anchor**

Completing your first thirteen weeks in this beautiful "Third Act" is a profound milestone. These initial turbulent months often involve wrestling with the void and deconstructing idols of productivity. Instead of focusing on lingering guilt or feeling unmoored, the wise Matriarch pauses to raise an Ebenezer.

This sacred reflection is not about measuring earthly success, but recognizing God's faithful help. Whether finding quiet afternoon peace or the strength to rest, the Lord has been your steady hand, graciously navigating you through this profound transition.

Reflection Questions

01   What is the most surprising thing you have learned about God in the silence of these first thirteen weeks?

02   Which "idol" of your professional life was the hardest to lay down?

03   Where do you see the "formless and empty" void of your first month beginning to take shape into a new calling?

Next Steps

☐ **The Physical Ebenezer:** Find a stone or a meaningful object and place it on your desk or nightstand as a reminder that God has helped you "up to this point."

☐ **The Quarterly Audit:** Reread your journaling from Week 1 and Week 13. Write down three specific ways your inner "voice" has changed.

Heavenly Father, I pause to stack these stones of gratitude. Thank You for Your help through these first thirteen weeks of transition. You have been my steady anchor in the midst of the void. Forgive my doubts and my restlessness. I look back at Your faithfulness and I find the courage to face the seasons ahead. Amen.

MILESTONE REVIEW

Congratulations, Matriarch. You have successfully navigated the first major threshold of your retirement journey. This section was designed to strip away the "worker" identity and reveal the "daughter" underneath. Before we move into Section 2, pause here for a collective review of y o u r progress.

Reflection Questions

01 Over the past thirteen weeks, what has been most difficult about ceasing from your professional labor?

02 How has your understanding of the Hebrew concept of Shabbat changed the way you view an empty calendar?

03 In which week did you feel the most significant shift from "clinging to status" to "accepting grace"?

Next Steps

☐ **Refining the Rule:** Take your "Preliminary Rule of Life" from Week 11 and refine it. What worked? What was too legalistic? Adjust it to better serve your soul for the next quarter.

☐ **The Legacy Letter:** Write a short letter to your younger "professional self." Explain to her why the "void" she feared is actually a sacred space for God's Spirit.

Heavenly Father, we thank You for the precision with which You have guided us through this first quarter. You have deconstructed our idols and crowned us with Your glory. As we move from the deconstruction of our old lives into the construction of our new calling, stay close to us. Help us to hold our boundaries with grace and to seek Your wisdom with all our strength. We are Your masterpieces, and we trust Your work. Amen.

02

THE MATRIARCH'S
HOLY BOUNDARIES

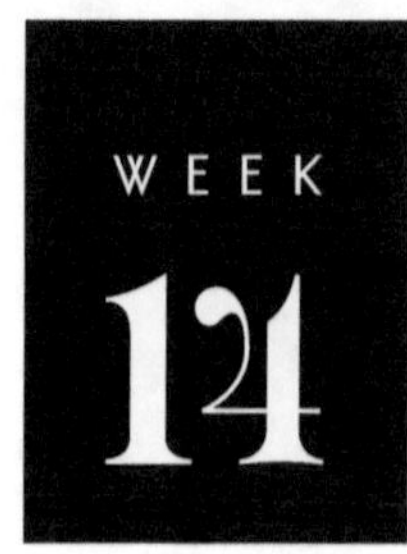

JESUS AT BETHANY

> As Jesus and the disciples were on their way, he came to a village where a woman named Martha opened her home to him. She had a sister called Mary, who sat at the Lord's feet listening to what he said. But Martha was distracted by all the preparations that had to be made. She came to him and asked, 'Lord, don't you care that my sister has left me to do the work by myself? Tell her to help me!' 'Martha, Martha,' the Lord answered, 'you are worried and upset about many things, but few things are needed—or indeed only one. Mary has chosen what is better, and it will not be taken away from her.
>
> — *Luke 10:38-42 (NLT)*

 **The Morning Anchor**

The Greek word *perispao* means being pulled in many directions. Once a professional badge of honor, this fragmented distraction is a barrier to the one thing Christ desires: you.

 **The Noon Anchor**

Retirement often replaces career schedules with endless social demands. Yet, Jesus establishes a profound boundary against this perispao. Your highest calling is no longer managing everyone's logistics, but choosing the better part at His feet. While stillness feels uncomfortable, the "doer" identity is temporary; only being with Him is eternal.

Reflection Questions

01 Where in your life do you currently feel pulled in different directions by others' expectations?

02 Why does sitting and listening feel harder or more guilt-filled than doing and serving?

03 What is the "one thing" you are currently neglecting because you are too worried about the "many things"?

Next Steps

☐ **The Bethany Boundary:** Identify one request for your time this week that would "distract" you from your spiritual rhythm and practice saying "no" with grace.

☐ **The Mary Hour:** Schedule a specific hour this week where the house may be "unprepared," but your soul is intentionally seated at the feet of Christ through scripture and silence.

Heavenly Father, I confess that I am often worried and upset about many things. Forgive me for allowing the demands of others to pull me away from Your presence. Today, I choose what is better. Help me to lay down my "preparations" and find my peace at Your feet. Let my identity be found in listening to Your voice rather than managing the world's noise. Amen.

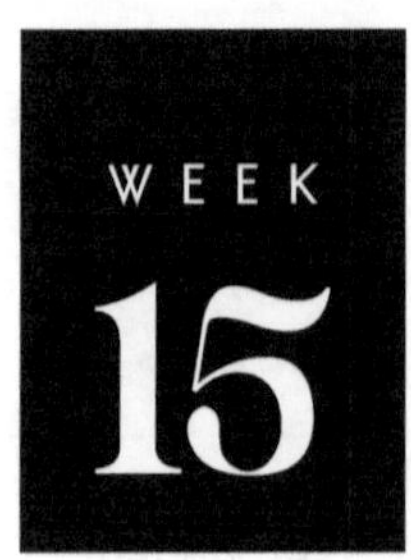

15

THE GRANDMOTHER BURNOUT

> Each time he said, 'My grace is all you need. My power works best in weakness.' So now I am glad to boast about my weaknesses, so that the power of Christ can work through me.
>
> — *2 Corinthians 12:9 (NLT)*

 **The Morning Anchor** 

The Greek word *charis* beautifully means grace—an unearned divine gift providing profound sufficiency when our natural strength fails. It is the sacred antidote to the exhausting "superwoman" myth, reminding us we need not be infinite because we serve an infinite Creator.

 **The Noon Anchor**

A silent epidemic often plagues retired women: the crushing weight of "Grandmother Burnout." Because of your competence, you are frequently treated as an inexhaustible resource, sacrificing your spiritual vitality for endless family demands. Yet, equating love with boundless labor is a profound theological error. You are called to be a wise Matriarch offering blessing, not a tireless laborer. Setting holy boundaries and admitting exhaustion is a beautiful surrender to charis. God's grace is wonderfully sufficient for your family, even when you humbly choose to rest.

Reflection Questions

01 How often do you say "yes" to childcare or family errands out of obligation instead of joy?

02 Do you feel admitting your physical or emotional exhaustion makes you a "bad" mother or grandmother?

03 How can you model "reliance on God's grace" to your family by admitting your own human limitations?

Next Steps

☐ **The Capacity Check:** Before agreeing to the next family request, wait twenty-four hours. Ask yourself if you have the physical and spiritual capacity to say "yes" without resentment.

☐ **The Grace Conversation:** Have an honest conversation with an adult child about your need for "refueling" time. Practice being clear about your boundaries without offering a dozen apologies.

Heavenly Father, I thank You that Your power works best in my weakness. Forgive me for trying to be everything to everyone and for neglecting the limits You have placed on my life. Help me to trust that Your grace is sufficient for my family when I cannot be there. Grant me the courage to set holy boundaries so that I may serve them out of love rather than exhaustion. Amen.

I

A FREE GIFT TO OUR READERS

BONUS

Love for your grandchildren should not
lead to the death of your spiritual life.

THE "GRANNY NANNY" BOUNDARY AGREEMENT

Inside, you'll find...

- Helps you intentionally transition from an "on-call servant" to a respected "spiritual elder".
- Supplies a fillable "Contract of Intent" to share with adult children to ensure clarity and prevent resentment.
- Establishes clear boundaries by detailing blackout dates for spiritual retreats, hard stop times, and legacy goals.

And more!

Download your FREE BONUS now!

https://mentalgrowthpublishing.com/retirement-devotional

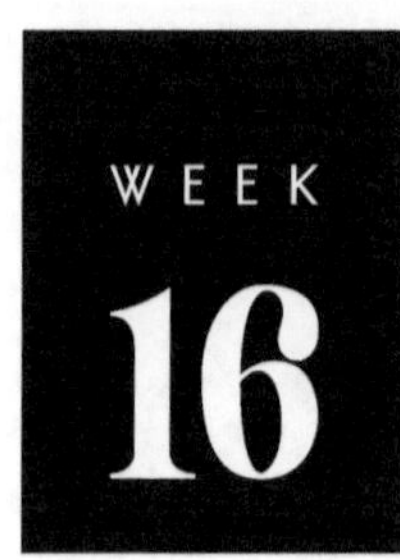

16

GEBUL: THE HOLINESS OF BORDERS

> Lord, you alone are my inheritance, my cup of blessing. You guard all that is mine. The boundary lines indicate a pleasant land; the property you have given me is beautiful.
>
> — *Psalm 16:5-6 (NLT)*

 **The Morning Anchor**

TThe Hebrew word gebul means a boundary marked by a cord. Moving a gebul was a serious ancient offense, violating God's assigned inheritance. These lines are not walls of isolation, but sacred markers defining where one person's stewardship faithfully ends.

 **The Noon Anchor**

In your career, a "scope of work" provided a clear gebul. In retirement, without that professional cord, these lines blur. Others often encroach on your "pleasant land," assuming your free time makes your life a public commons. But the psalmist calls boundaries a blessing, not selfishness. God guards your peace, time, and primary calling. Allowing others to move your gebul abandons the beautiful property God assigned you. A Matriarch cannot lead from wisdom if her life is constantly trampled. Holy boundaries protect your fruitful legacy. Your land is beautiful, Matriarch. Keep the lines clear.

Reflection Questions

01 Where have the "boundary lines" of your life been moved by the expectations or demands of others?

02 Do you view boundaries as "unpleasant" walls or as "pleasant" markers of your Godgiven inheritance?

03 What "beautiful property" (a hobby, a prayer time, a rest period) in your life has been trampled by distractions?

Next Steps

☐ **The Cord Ceremony:** Spend time in prayer asking God to help you "mark out your territory." Write down three nonnegotiable boundaries for your current season.

☐ **The Guarded Land:** Choose one morning this week to be "unreachable." Turn off your phone and guard the boundary of your peace with the Lord.

Heavenly Father, I thank You for the pleasant land You have given me to inhabit. Forgive me for allowing others to move my boundary lines and for neglecting the stewardship of my time. Help me to reclaim my gebul with grace and strength. Guard my inheritance and teach me to find beauty in the limits You have set for my life. Amen.

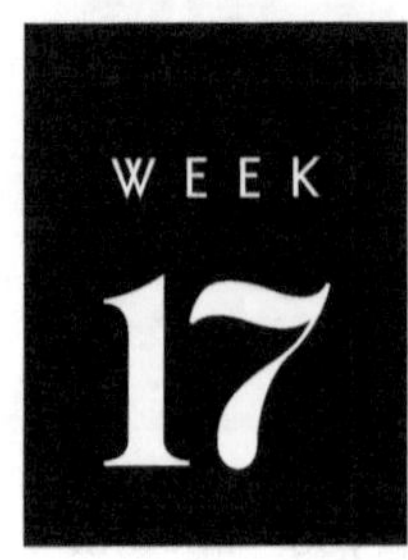

THE SILENCE OF ESTRANGEMENT

> Even if my father and mother abandon me, the Lord will hold me close.
>
> — *Psalm 27:10 (NLT)*

The Morning Anchor

The Hebrew word *acaph* beautifully means to be gathered in or held close. Like a tender shepherd rescuing a left-behind lamb, it is a restorative promise. When earthly relationships fail or fade into silence, God intentionally gathers you into His divine embrace.

The Noon Anchor

A profound agony in retirement is the ambiguous loss of family estrangement. Instead of a joyful legacy gathering, you may face the shameful silence of broken bonds, burdened by cultural whispers of parental failure. Yet, the theology of acaph beautifully rewrites this pain. When foundational human connections sever, God does not shame you; He gently gathers you into His arms.

Surrender this painful silence to the Father, finally releasing all frantic self-blame. Your infinite worth is eternally anchored in His perfect love, not in earthly approval. You are not rejected; you are beautifully, tenderly held.

Reflection Questions

01 How has the "shame of silence" from a family member changed the way you view your own spiritual identity?

02 In what ways are you still trying to "earn" reconciliation through self-blame or a loss of boundaries?

03 How can you find comfort in the acaph of God while you wait in the "wilderness" of family silence?

Next Steps

☐ **The Shame Surrender:** Write down the names of the family members from whom you are estranged. Pray over each name, consciously handing the "shame of the silence" back to God and accepting His gathering embrace.

☐ **The New Gathering:** Identify one person in your life (a friend, a younger believer, or a neighbor) who needs "holding close." Practice the acaph of God by offering them a small gesture of belonging.

Heavenly Father, I bring the pain of my family silence to You. Forgive me for taking the shame of estrangement upon myself. I thank You that even if I feel abandoned by those I love, You will hold me close. Gather me into Your house of belonging today. Heal the wounds of rejection and let me find my peace in Your gathering embrace. Amen.

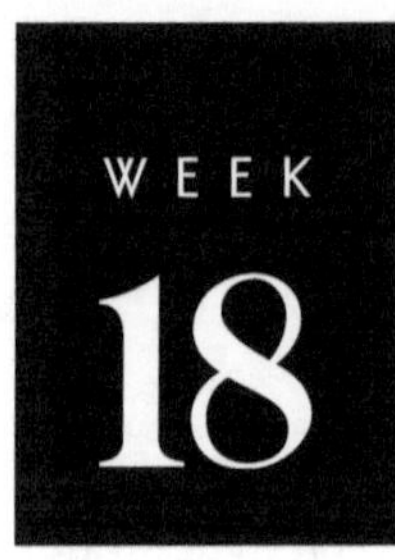

18

GRIEVING THE LIVING

> The Lord is close to the brokenhearted; he rescues those whose spirits are crushed. The righteous person faces many troubles, but the Lord comes to the rescue each time.
>
> — *Psalm 34:18-19 (NLT)*

The Morning Anchor

The Hebrew word *shabar* beautifully describes a shattered, broken heart—a deep, structural break of relational expectations. Yet, God being close means He intentionally inhabits these very cracks. He provides a divine adhesive that does not hide your brokenness, but powerfully sanctifies it.

The Noon Anchor

A profound grief in the Third Act is mourning the living. When your cherished script of family gatherings shatters, you experience a crushed, ambiguous sorrow, grieving a relationship absent in substance. You managed complex careers; surely you can fix family dynamics. Yet, people are not projects. Grieving the living requires surrendering the control you once wielded professionally. You must mourn the family you expected, to eventually love the family you have. God does not demand you fix this brokenness; He promises to be intimately close. Your worth is not determined by your adult children's choices.

Reflection Questions

01   What specific "script" or expectation for your family life are you currently grieving?

02   How has your habit of "fixing things" made it harder to accept a broken relationship?

03   In what ways can you feel the Lord being "close" to the specific shattered pieces of your heart today?

Next Steps

☐ **The Expectation Burial:** Write down one specific expectation you had for your retirement family life that has not come true. Pray over it and "bury" it, asking God to help you let go of the pain of that loss.

☐ **The Broken Beauty:** Find a piece of pottery or a photo of a repaired item. Keep it near you this week as a visual reminder that God works in the shattered places.

Heavenly Father, I bring the shattered pieces of my heart to You today. Forgive me for trying to fix people and situations that are beyond my control. I thank You for Your promise to be close to the brokenhearted. Rescue me from the weight of unrealized expectations and the shame of family rejection. Help me to find my wholeness in Your presence alone. Amen.

THE INVISIBLE WOMAN

> *Thereafter, Hagar used another name to refer to the Lord, who had spoken to her. She said, 'You are the God who sees me.' She also said, 'Have I truly seen the One who sees me?*
>
> — *Genesis 16:13 (NLT)*

 **The Morning Anchor**

The Hebrew name *El Roi* translates to "The God who sees." The root ra'ah means to perceive, consider, and provide. For the retired woman feeling culturally invisible, being the subject of this divine attention is your beautiful, saving theological anchor.

 **The Noon Anchor**

In your career, your expertise commanded visibility. Retirement often brings a devastating "invisibility syndrome," leaving you feeling like society simply looks right through you. Accustomed to the dopamine of professional recognition, you may frantically shout into the void to prove you still matter. Yet, we must beautifully counter this profound pain with the comforting theology of El Roi. The world values youth and outward productivity, but the Father intimately perceives your hard-won wisdom. This cultural invisibility is actually a sacred invitation to finally stop performing. You are deeply perceived by the God who sees you.

01   In what specific environments do you feel most "invisible" or overlooked lately?

02   How much of your current activity is driven by a desperate need to "be seen" or "prove" your relevance?

03   How does the name El Roi change your perspective on a day spent entirely in "hidden" or quiet service?

Next Steps

The Secret Service: Perform one act of kindness or service this week that no one will ever know about. Enjoy the private secret between you and El Roi.

The Gaze Practice: Spend ten minutes each day sitting in silence, consciously "looking up" to the God who sees you. Practice simply being the subject of His love without performing any task.

Heavenly Father, I thank You that You are the God who sees me. Forgive me for my obsession with worldly visibility and my fear of becoming irrelevant. Help me to find my security in Your gaze alone. Let me be content to be hidden in You, knowing that my value is perceived and provided for by Your grace. Amen.

MARRIAGE RECALIBRATION

> And I ask you, my true partner, to help these two women, for they worked hard with me in telling others the Good News. They worked along with Clement and the rest of my co-workers, whose names are written in the Book of Life.
>
> — *Philippians 4:3 (NLT)*

The Morning Anchor

The Greek word *syzygos* means "yokefellow," illustrating two oxen pulling a common load. In long-term marriage, it beautifully describes recalibrating roles when career and parenting yokes vanish. It is the profound transition from merely working apart to truly living together.

The Noon Anchor

Retirement is often your marriage's greatest stress test. For decades, you were yoked to separate careers, managing household logistics in the margins. Now, without professional buffers, you face each other constantly, risking mutual irritation as independent professionals clash in shared spaces. You must navigate a profound syzygos recalibration. Avoid the temptation to supervise your spouse like an employee to regain lost workplace control. Instead, the Third Act calls you to beautifully find a new shared yoke, perhaps a ministry or legacy project. Stop managing, start walking together, and bravely pull toward the Kingdom as partners.

Reflection Questions

01 Where is friction most present in your home, and how much stems from career management habits?

02 What "third party" once mediated your relationship, and how are you coping now without it?

03 What "common load" or spiritual goal could you and your spouse pull together this season?

Next Steps

☐ **The Role Negotiation:** Sit down with your spouse and have a clear, "business-style" meeting about your home logistics. Who owns which space? How much "alone time" does each person need? Be direct and gracious.

☐ **The Partner Prayer:** Commit to praying with your spouse for five minutes each day this week. Use this time to ask God to help you be "true partners" in this new season.

Heavenly Father, I thank You for the partner You have given me. Forgive me for my impatience and my desire to control our shared space. Help us to recalibrate our marriage for this Third Act. Teach us to be true syzygos, yoked together in Your service and pulling toward Your Kingdom with one heart. Amen.

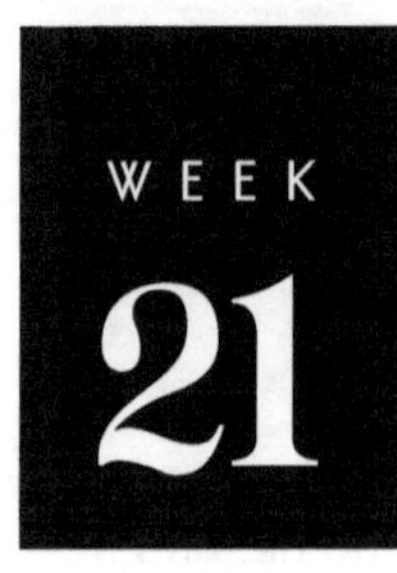

THE WHOLENESS OF BEING ALONE

> Let all that I am wait quietly before God, for my hope is in him.
>
> — *Psalm 62:5 (NLT)*

The Morning Anchor

The Hebrew word *dumiyyah* means waiting quietly in silent expectation and trusting repose in God. For the woman navigating retirement alone, removing workplace noise beautifully allows the soul to find its undivided hope and complete wholeness anchored in the Father.

The Noon Anchor

Retirement can be a lonely landscape for the woman navigating it without a partner. Whether widowed, divorced, or single, leaving the workplace removes the daily social noise that once masked your solitude. When working, you belonged to a team; now, the silence of your house might feel like a verdict of not being enough. Our couple-centric culture often makes single retirees feel like missing fragments. Counter this fear with the beautiful theology of dumiyyah. Wholeness is found in quiet, singular expectation of God. You are not a half waiting to be made whole. You are a complete child of God. Your solitude offers a unique capacity for undivided waiting, Matriarch.

Reflection Questions

01 In what specific moments does your solo status make you feel "fragmented" or "incomplete"?

02 How can you transform your solitude into a "silent expectation" of God's presence this week?

03 What is the primary source of your hope right now, and is it rooted more in human or divine connection?

Next Steps

☐ **The Silence Liturgy:** If you live alone, treat one evening this week as a formal "time of waiting." Turn off the lights, light a candle, and sit in absolute dumiyyah for fifteen minutes, allowing your soul to rest in God.

☐ **The Hope List:** Write down three reasons why being "undivided" in this season is a spiritual advantage for your specific calling or legacy.

Heavenly Father, I thank You that my wholeness is found in You alone. Forgive me for feeling incomplete or fragmented because of my solo status. I choose to wait quietly before You today. Let my hope be anchored in Your unchanging love. Teach me the peace of dumiyyah and help me to find my unity in Your presence. Amen.

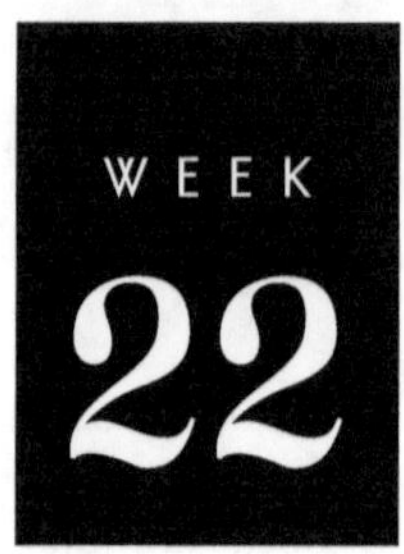

THE STEWARDSHIP OF ENERGY

> *He gives power to the weak and strength to the powerless. Even youths will become weak and tired, and young men will fall in exhaustion. But those who trust in the Lord will find new strength. They will soar high on wings like eagles. They will run and not grow weary. They will walk and not faint.*
>
> — *Isaiah 40:29-31 (NLT)*

 **The Morning Anchor**

The Hebrew word *koach* signifies physical strength and capacity. For the Matriarch, this vigor is now a finite resource. Unlike the boundless energy of youth, your Third Act koach is a daily, managed currency graciously received from the Lord alone.

 **The Noon Anchor**

In your career, you pushed through fatigue, treating energy as an unlimited resource summoned by sheer will. In retirement, your physical body humbly signals new limits. Refusing these natural boundaries essentially declares your earthly work more important than God's beautiful design for rest. A wise Matriarch understands her koach is now a sacred budget. You cannot say yes to every demand and still retain strength to pray deeply or mentor wisely. Stop apologizing for your fatigue. By making hard stewardship choices, you discover profound, new vigor, found not in willpower, but in waiting upon God.

01 In what areas of your life are you currently "spending" your energy on things that do not bear eternal fruit?

02 How do your physical limits confront your professional ego, and how can you receive it with grace?

03 What would it mean to receive your daily koach from the Lord instead of manufacturing it yourself?

Next Steps

☐ **The Energy Audit:** For three days this week, rate your energy levels on a scale of 1 to 10 at morning, noon, and evening. Identify which activities "drain" your koach and which "refill" it.

☐ **The Sacred Nap:** Intentionally schedule a period of rest during the day when you would normally feel the urge to "push through." Treat this rest as a spiritual discipline of trust.

Heavenly Father, I thank You that You give power to the weak. Forgive me for trying to operate out of my own strength and for neglecting the limits of the body You have given me. Help me to steward my energy with wisdom and intentionality. Teach me to wait on You for the koach I need for this day, and let me find my rest in Your sufficiency. Amen.

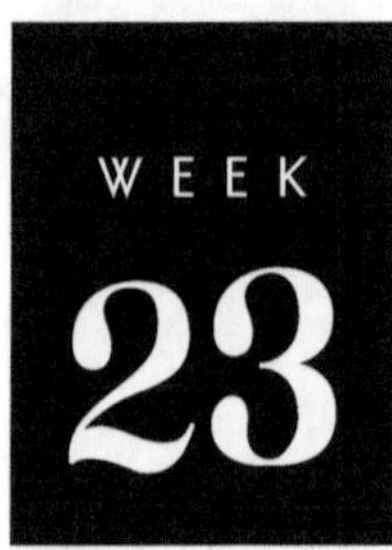

23

THE WISDOM OF "NO"

> Just say a simple, 'Yes, I will,' or 'No, I won't.' Anything beyond this is from the evil one.
>
> — *Matthew 5:37 (NLT)*

 **The Morning Anchor** 

The Greek words *nai* (yes) and *ou* (no) call for radical simplicity of speech reflecting profound soul clarity. For the professional woman, these words are sacred boundary markers preventing resentful commitments and beautifully eliminating the burden of guilt.

 **The Noon Anchor**

For decades, your reliable "yes" was the engine of your success. In retirement, this habit becomes a liability. Because people perceive your time as free, they flood you with requests. Without the wisdom of a simple, unqualified "no," your life quickly becomes a disorganized collection of other people's priorities.

A Matriarch does not need to justify her boundaries with defensive explanations rooted in a fear of displeasing others. A holy "no" to a distraction is a profound "yes" to your true calling, beautifully protecting the sacred legacy work God has designed for your Third Act.

Reflection Questions

01 Why do you feel the need to offer an explanation or an excuse every time you have to say "no" to a request?

02 What specific "yes" in your life right now is actually producing resentment in your soul?

03 How would your peace change if a simple "no" were enough to preserve your worth in others' eyes?

Next Steps

The Unqualified No: Identify one request this week that you want to decline. Practice saying, "No, I am not able to do that at this time," without offering a single reason why. Observe the urge to "over-explain" and let it pass.

The Priority Filter: Write down the three "big yeses" of your retirement season. Before saying "yes" to anything else this week, ask if it supports or distracts from these three priorities.

Heavenly Father, I thank You for the clarity of Your Word. Forgive me for my people- pleasing and my fear of being seen as unavailable. Help me to let my "yes" be "yes" and my "no" be "no." Grant me the wisdom to say "no" to the distractions that drain my soul so that I may say "yes" to the calling You have for me. Amen.

A FREE GIFT TO OUR READERS

BONUS

You spent decades saying "yes" to bosses and clients; now you are saying "yes" to everyone else but God.

THE "HOLY NO" SCRIPT VAULT

defending your shabbat

Inside, you'll find...

- Provides the exact words to decline commitments without the weight of "good girl" guilt.
- Equips you with 15 specific scripts to handle church committees, overreaching family members, and high-demand volunteer roles.
- Anchors your boundaries in a "Theology of Limits" preamble based on the biblical concept of Gebu

And more!

Download your FREE BONUS now!

https://mentalgrowthpublishing.com/retirement-devotional

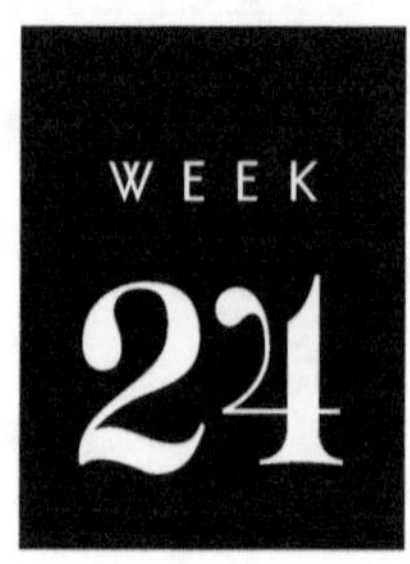

FINANCIAL ANXIETY AND RADICAL TRUST

> That is why I tell you not to worry about everyday life—whether you have enough food and drink, or enough clothes to wear. Isn't life more than food, and your body more than clothing? Look at the birds. They don't plant or harvest or store food in barns, for your heavenly Father feeds them. And aren't you far more valuable to him than they are?
>
> — *Matthew 6:25-26 (NLT)*

 **The Morning Anchor**

The Greek word *merimnao* means to worry, describing a soul drawn in different directions. This mental fragmentation occurs when we try securing our future through anxiety, losing our singular focus of trust. It suggests our mind is playing the Provider.

 **The Noon Anchor**

Retirement often brings the quiet terror of financial anxiety. Without a paycheck, relying on savings sparks fears of outliving your resources. This merimnao challenges your belief in your value to the Father. Jesus gently reminds us that birds lack barns, yet are faithfully fed. Your earthly career was simply God's temporary delivery system; your ultimate security was never in a 401k. The Provider remains unchanged. Embrace radical trust, shifting from self-reliance to God-reliance. You are wonderfully cared for, Matriarch; the Father knows your every need.

Reflection Questions

01 How much of your peace rests on your bank balance rather than God's promises?

02 In what ways is financial anxiety "dividing" your mind and distracting you from your current calling?

03 If you truly believed you are more valuable than the birds, how would your spending and giving change?

Next Steps

☐ **The Provision List:** Write down five times in your professional life when God provided for a need in an unexpected way. Keep this list in your wallet as a reminder of His track record.

☐ **The Trust Gift:** Identify a small way you can be generous this week (a donation, a gift to a neighbor, a meal for someone). Practice the "release" of resources as an act of trust in the Father's ongoing provision.

Heavenly Father, I confess that I often worry about my future and my finances. Forgive me for my lack of trust and for my attempt to find my security in my own barns. I thank You that I am valuable to You. Help me to look at the birds and remember Your faithfulness. I choose to trust You as my Provider today and for all the days to come. Amen.

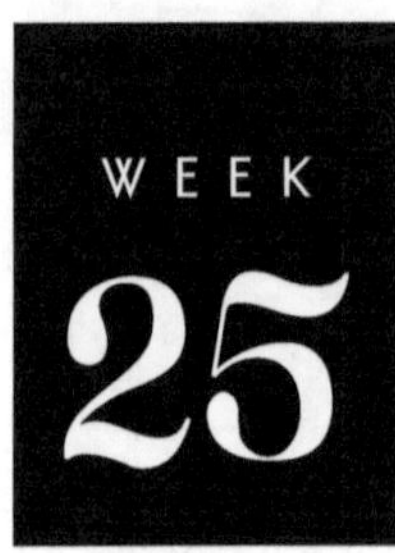

25

RELATIONAL LEGACY

> 
> And you must commit yourselves wholeheartedly to these commands that I am giving you today. Repeat them again and again to your children. Talk about them when you are at home and when you are on the road, when you are going to bed and when you are getting up.
>
> — *Deuteronomy 6:6-7 (NLT)*

 **The Morning Anchor** 

The Hebrew word *shanan* means to diligently teach or sharpen, like a sword on a whetstone. It is a persistent, intentional refining of character. For the Matriarch, it marks the beautiful transition from merely managing children to intentionally sharpening grand-generations.

 **The Noon Anchor**

In your career and early parenting, legacy meant successful projects and safe children. In retirement, you must transition from managing to mentoring. Controlling your adult children now only produces friction. Instead, cultivate a beautiful atmosphere of wisdom. A Matriarch carries the sharpening stone of decades of experience, offering a whetstone of truth rather than demanding obedience. You naturally sharpen the next generation through how you live, pray, and hold holy boundaries. Stop frantically managing outcomes; start intentionally modeling character. Keep your own sword sharp.

Reflection Questions

01 In what areas are you trying to "manage" adult children rather than "sharpening" them through wisdom?

02 What is the "spiritual scent" or the primary message that you are currently leaving in your family home?

03 How can you "talk about God's truth" in a natural, noncontrolling way during your next family interaction?

Next Steps

☐ **The Wisdom Offering:** Instead of offering "advice" to a family member this week, offer a "story of God's faithfulness" from your own life. Focus on the testimony rather than the instruction.

☐ **The Legacy Blessing:** Write a short, handwritten note to a grandchild or a younger relative. Specifically name one "godly command" or trait you see in them and "sharpen" them with your encouragement.

Heavenly Father, I thank You for the family You have placed me in. Forgive me for my desire to control and manage those I love. Help me to commit myself wholeheartedly to Your truth. Teach me to be a "sharpening stone" for the next generation. Let my legacy be one of wisdom, love, and a persistent presence of Your Spirit. Amen.

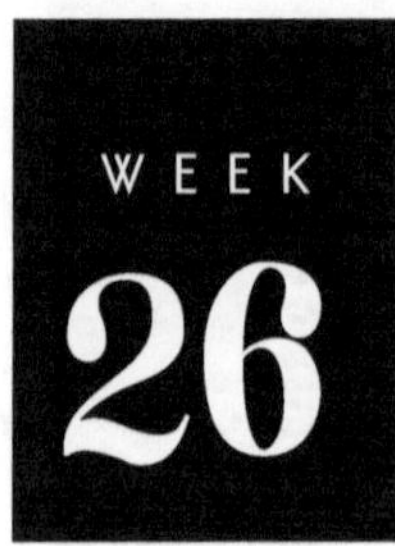

THE MID-YEAR ANCHOR

> The faithful love of the Lord never ends! His mercies begin afresh each morning.
>
> — *Lamentations 3:22-23 (NLT)*

 **The Morning Anchor**

The Hebrew words *chesed* and *chadash* mean faithful love and new restoration. At this six-month mark, chadash chesed beautifully promises God isn't weary of your profound transition. His resetting mercy is not a finite resource but an endless morning fountain.

 **The Noon Anchor**

You have reached the halfway point of your Year of Refirement. For twenty-six weeks, you architected a new existence, deconstructing professional ego and learning the radical wisdom of "no." Most importantly, you inhabited your Matriarch identity. This Mid-Year Anchor beautifully pauses to reveal God's daily mercies are gifts, not rewards for successful retirement. Can you see His chesed in your strength to decline exhausting obligations or in quiet solitude? Retirement often feels like running out of relevance, yet you are running into an endless mercy fountain. Just receive His chadash love at sunrise, holy Matriarch.

Reflection Questions

01 In what area of your retirement transition do you feel you have "run out" of patience or grace lately?

02 How do "mercies beginning afresh" change your perspective on the last six months of missteps or drift?

03 What is the most significant evidence of God's chesed (faithful love) that you have experienced since Week 1?

Next Steps

☐ **The Mercy Inventory:** Write down three specific "mercies" from the first half of the year that you never expected to receive.

☐ **The Morning Reset:** For the next seven days, wake up and immediately speak the words: "His mercies are new for me today." Observe how this resets your internal "worker bee" anxiety.

Heavenly Father, I thank You that Your faithful love never ends. Forgive me for my fear of running out of grace and my attempt to earn Your favor through my transition. I thank You for the mercies that begin afresh for me this morning. Help me to inhabit the second half of this year with a joyful heart, knowing that You are my unshakeable Provider. Amen.

MILESTONE REVIEW

You have successfully completed the second quarter of your journey. This section was designed to help you protect the "Beautiful Property" of your retirement from the encroachment of worldly expectations. Before we move into Section 3, pause here to evaluate the health of your boundary lines.

Reflection Questions

01 Which "Holy Boundary" was the most difficult for you to set (Family, Church, or Social Obligations), and why?

02 How has the concept of El Roi (The God who sees) reshaped your experience of "invisibility" in retirement?

03 In what ways has the "recalibration" of your marriage or your singleness produced a new sense of wholeness in your home?

The Boundary Audit: Identify one person or organization that still consistently tries to "move your boundary lines." Draft a gracious, clear statement of your "no" for the next time they ask.

The Rest Evaluation: Are you still struggling with "Grandmother Burnout" or energy depletion? Adjust your schedule for the next quarter to prioritize the stewardship of your koach.

Heavenly Father, we thank You for the protection of Your boundary lines. You have taught us that our time and our energy are holy resources to be guarded for Your glory. Forgive us for our people-pleasing and our fear of being seen as "useless." As we move into the deeper theology of the next quarter, keep our lands pleasant and our hearts focused on You. We trust You to guard all that is ours. Amen.

03

THE MIND OF THE MATRIARCH

THE ANCIENT OF DAYS

> As I watched, thrones were put in place and the Ancient One sat down to judge. His clothing was as white as snow, his hair like purest wool. He sat on a fiery throne with wheels of blazing fire.
>
> — *Daniel 7:9 (NLT)*

The Morning Anchor

The Aramaic title *Atiq Yomin*, "The Ancient of Days," means enduring and removed from ordinary time. It reveals a God untouched by decay. While we often view aging as fading, Atiq Yomin beautifully reminds us that true wisdom increases with our days.

The Noon Anchor

For decades, your career demanded exhausting innovation and agility. Now, anchor your identity in the Atiq Yomin. While culture obsesses over youth, God's "hair like purest wool" reveals your silver hair as a beautiful reflection of His eternal character. Your years are not a liability; they invite deeper resonance with enduring truth.

Stop apologizing for advanced age. You are not obsolete; you are being refined into a visible testament of the God who beautifully endures. Sit on your throne of experience, Matriarch.

Reflection Questions

01 How does the title "Ancient of Days" challenge the cultural lie that aging is a loss of value or relevance?

02 How have you shaped your faith to keep up with cultural speed rather than resting in God's unchanging nature?

03 How do you model the "weight" and "splendor" of the Ancient One to youth terrified of growing old?

Next Steps

☐ **The Eternal View:** Spend twenty minutes this week studying the visions of God in Daniel 7 and Revelation 4. Contrast the "blazing fire" of His throne with the "fading spark" of worldly trends.

☐ **The Wisdom Declaration:** Identify one truth about God that you have known for over forty years. Write it down and share it with someone this week as a testament to the God who does not change.

Heavenly Father, I thank You that You are the Ancient of Days. Forgive me for my fear of the passing years and my obsession with being "new" and "relevant." I choose to anchor my soul in Your enduring authority. Let my silver hair be a crown of honor that reflects Your eternal nature. Teach me to walk with the dignity of one who belongs to the Ancient One. Amen.

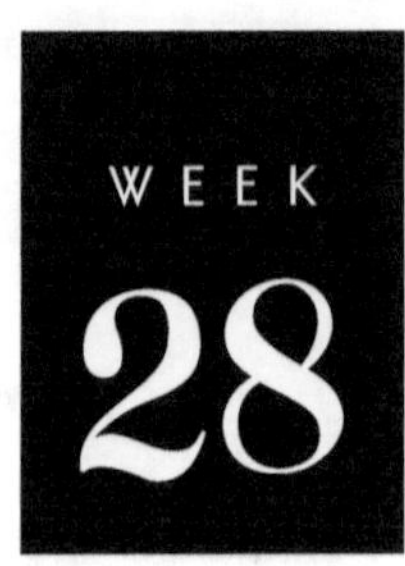

SYSTEMATIC THEOLOGY OF SUFFERING

> For our present troubles are small and won't last very long. Yet they produce for us a glory that vastly outweighs them and will last forever! So we don't look at the troubles we can see now; rather, we fix our gaze on things that cannot be seen.
>
> — *2 Corinthians 4:17-18 (NLT)*

 **The Morning Anchor**

The Greek word *thlipsis* beautifully describes troubles as pressure—a crushing or squeezing that narrows your path, like pressing olives for oil. This is no accidental tragedy, but purposeful pressure. The Father uses this crushing to extract your life's most valuable fruit.

 **The Noon Anchor**

We often expect retirement to be smooth sailing, feeling we earned comfort. When chronic pain or declining independence arrives instead, we struggle to reconcile the "Golden Years" myth with reality. Yet, God never wastes your pressure. These present troubles are not interruptions, but the curriculum of your maturity. This purposeful thlipsis squeezes out the beautiful oil of your character—patience, trust, and deep peace. You are not being crushed to be destroyed, Matriarch; you are being pressed to be poured out as a blessing.

Reflection Questions

01 What specific "pressure" (thlipsis) currently feels like it is narrowing your possibilities?

02 How do you shift your gaze from visible troubles (pain, loss, loneliness) to God's internal "weight of glory"?

03 In what ways has suffering made your spiritual life more "weighty" than in your comfortable years?

Next Steps

☐ **The Glory Weight Audit:** List three "fruits" that have grown in your soul specifically because of a hard season in the last year (e.g., deeper prayer life, increased empathy, radical trust).

☐ **The Lament and Praise:** Write a "Lament of the Pressed." Honestly tell God where it hurts, but end the prayer by specifically naming one "unseen" glory you are fixing your gaze on.

Heavenly Father, I bring the weight of my current troubles to You. Forgive me for my resentment of the pressure and my desire for a life of shallow comfort. I thank You that You are using this thlipsis to produce an eternal glory in me. Help me to fix my gaze on the things that cannot be seen. Let the oil of Your Spirit flow from my life even in the midst of the crushing. Amen.

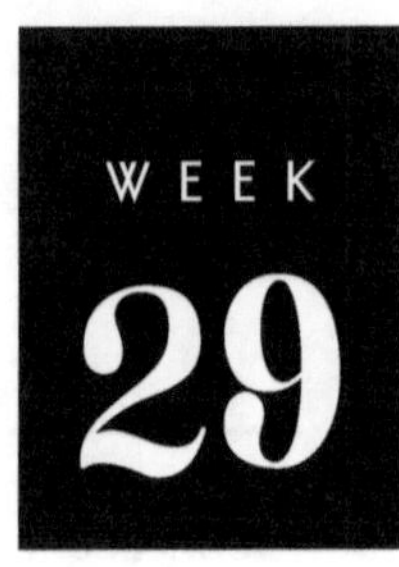

29

ANANEOO: THE RENEWAL OF THE MIND

> Instead, let the Spirit renew your thoughts and attitudes.
>
> — *Ephesians 4:23 (NLT)*

The Morning Anchor

The Greek word *ananeoo* means to renew or restore to an original state. More than a superficial coat of paint, it implies deep, structural renovation. The Spirit beautifully performs this ananeoo on our minds, replacing old professional logic with eternal Kingdom perspective.

The Noon Anchor

For decades in your career, your mind was strictly trained in the rigid logic of efficiency, competition, and total reliance on yourself. In retirement, this outdated framework often leads to stale, repetitive thinking. You may find yourself anxiously ruminating on past professional slights or worrying about current irrelevance. Therefore, a Kingdom Matriarch requires a radical ananeoo.

This profound spiritual renewal is not merely thinking positive thoughts; it is a complete structural renovation of your intellectual house by the Holy Spirit. As you bravely shift away from worldly protection toward holy direction, your mind ceases being a dusty storage unit for professional ghosts and becomes a beautiful, abiding sanctuary.

Reflection Questions

01 What specific old thought, such as bitterness or the need to control, is the Spirit trying to renovate in you?

02 How can you differentiate a Spirit-renovated thought from the stale logic of your former career?

03 In what area would a renewed attitude produce the most significant change in your peace this week?

Next Steps

The Mental Renovation: Identify one stale attitude you have held lately. Spend ten minutes in prayer, specifically asking the Spirit to ananeoo that specific thought.

The Fresh Perspective: Read one chapter of scripture that you have read many times before. Ask the Spirit to show you something new or original in the text, treating it as a fresh renovation of your mind.

Heavenly Father, I thank You that Your Spirit is at work in my mind. Forgive me for clinging to old professional logic and stale attitudes. I choose to let You renovate my thinking today. Strip away the outdated frameworks of my past and reveal the fresh perspective of Your Kingdom. Let my thoughts be a sanctuary for Your truth. Amen.

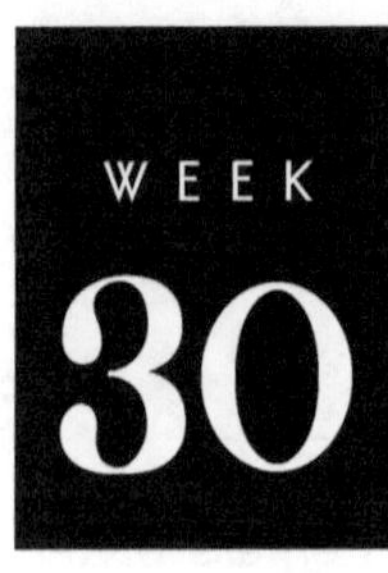

30 FAITH SHIFTING IN THE THIRD ACT

> This means that all of creation will be shaken and removed, so that only unshakeable things will remain. Since we are receiving a Kingdom that is unshakeable, let us be thankful and please God by worshiping him with holy fear and awe.
>
> — Hebrews 12:27-28 (NLT)

 **The Morning Anchor**

The Greek word *saleuo* means to be shaken, tottering like a building in an earthquake. This profound agitation tests your foundation. In later life, spiritual "earthquakes" test long-held dogmas. Yet, this divine shaking doesn't destroy; it beautifully reveals what is truly unshakeable.

 **The Noon Anchor**

You may enter retirement expecting your faith to be perfectly settled. Yet, the Third Act often brings profound "faith shifting." Facing the void of retirement and the hard questions of aging, long-held dogmas undergo a saleuo earthquake. This shaking feels like a spiritual crisis, but it is actually divine mercy. God allows the shaking of temporary, borrowed religiosity so that only unshakeable things remain. Do not panic when your faith wavers, Matriarch. You are not losing your faith; you are clearing the clutter to finally discover the eternal, unshakeable Rock of Christ beneath it all.

01 What specific "shaking" are you currently experiencing in your health, your family, or your belief system?

02 How do you distinguish "losing your faith" from "removing shakeable things" in your foundation?

03 What are the three "unshakeable things" in your life that remain constant even when everything else is tottering?

Next Steps

The Unshakeable List: Write down five things about God and His Kingdom that you know are absolutely true, regardless of your current circumstances. Keep this list as your "foundation report."

The Honest Inquiry: Identify one theological question you have been "shaking" over. Instead of hiding it, spend time researching it in a deep, intellectual commentary this week.

Heavenly Father, I thank You for the unshakeable Kingdom I am receiving. Forgive me for my fear when the things I once relied on begin to totter. I choose to trust the shaking. Remove the temporary and the fragile from my faith so that only Your eternal truth remains. Help me to worship You with holy fear and awe in the midst of the storm. Amen.

THE DIGITAL SABBATH

> Then Jesus said, 'Let's go off by ourselves to a quiet place and rest awhile.' He said this because there were so many people coming and going that Jesus and his apostles didn't even have time to eat.
>
> — Mark 6:31 (NLT)

The Morning Anchor

The Greek word *hesychia* means quiet stillness, a profound tranquility free from external and internal agitation. Early Christians considered this purposeful withdrawal into a singular focus the prerequisite for deep prayer. For the retiree, it is a holy boundary against digital noise.

The Noon Anchor

As a professional, you consumed information to stay relevant. In retirement, this often mutates into a compulsive digital attachment. Endlessly scrolling through global anxieties fragments your soul. You are retired from your job, yet enslaved to the screen's false urgency. This constant consumption prevents the profound hesychia required to hear the Spirit. You are mentally exhausted by the trivial, leaving you spiritually malnourished for the eternal. A Matriarch knows her attention is a holy resource. Practice the discipline of digital withdrawal. Turn off notifications to finally hear the whisper of the One holding the world.

01 How many daily hours do you spend "scrolling" information with no impact on your life or calling?

02 What specific "global anxiety" are you currently carrying that belongs to the Father rather than your own heart?

03 How would your internal hesychia change if you committed to a weekly 24-hour "Digital Sabbath"?

Next Steps

☐ **The Notification Fast:** Turn off all nonessential notifications on your phone this week. Reclaim the "right of first entry" to your own mind.

☐ **The Solitary Walk:** Go for a twenty-minute walk without your phone. Practice being "by yourself" in a quiet place, observing the world with your own eyes rather than through a screen.

Heavenly Father, I confess that I have allowed the noise of the world to crowd out Your voice. Forgive me for my addiction to information and my fear of being "out of the loop." I choose to seek the hesychia of Your presence today. Help me to lay down my digital burdens and to find my rest in the quiet place You have prepared for me. Amen.

THE SUMMER SLUMP

> So let's not get tired of doing what is good. At just the right
> time we will reap a harvest of blessing if we don't give up.
>
> — *Galatians 6:9 (NLT)*

The Morning Anchor

The Greek word *ekluō* means to faint, describing a bowstring losing its tension. Without tension, it cannot propel arrows. For the retiree, this ekluō is a spiritual "Summer Slump"— collapsing into aimless relaxation after decades of tight professional demands.

The Noon Anchor

For decades, your career required constant, exhausting tension. In retirement, removing this daily pressure often triggers a radical slackening—a dangerous "Summer Slump" of the soul. This *ekluō* is not holy rest; it is letting your spirit become limp, tempted by endless passive consumption. A permanent loss of internal tension endangers your higher calling. A Kingdom Matriarch knows a slack bowstring is useless, but one under holy tension is an instrument of divine precision. Transition beautifully to Kingdom tension. Stay fiercely engaged in prayer and mentorship. Do not let your bowstring go slack, Matriarch; you still have powerful arrows of wisdom to propel into the next generation.

Reflection Questions

01 Where in your spiritual life do you feel Ekluō—a desire to "just vanish" from responsibility?

02 How does a "slackened bowstring" describe your current engagement with the Kingdom of God?

03 What is the difference between "holy rest" and "purposeful tension" in your current weekly schedule?

Next Steps

☐ **The Tension Check:** Identify one spiritual discipline you have recently "dropped" because you felt you had "done enough." Ask God if this slackening is a healthy rest or a dangerous Ekluō.

☐ **The Harvest Focus:** Write down one specific "good thing" you are currently doing (e.g., intercession, checking on a neighbor). Commit to doing it with fresh intentionality this week, refusing to let your grip slacken.

Heavenly Father, I thank You that Your work in me is never finished. Forgive me for the times my heart has become limp and I have wanted to give up on my calling. Restore the holy tension of my soul today. Strengthen my hands for the specific good You have for me in this season. Help me to stay engaged with Your Spirit so that I may reap the harvest You have prepared for my later years. Amen.

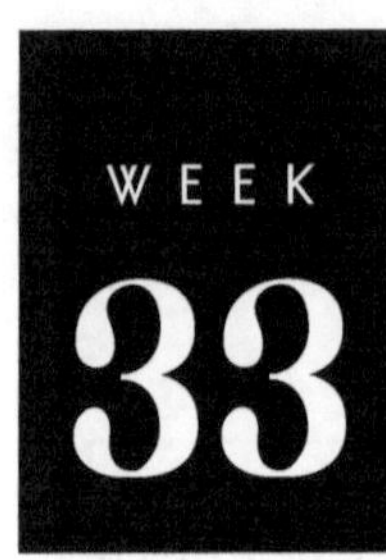

33

SOPHIA: THE SKILL OF LIVING

> *If you need wisdom, ask our generous God, and he will give it to you. He will not rebuke you for asking.*
>
> — *James 1:5 (NLT)*

The Morning Anchor

The Greek word *Sophia* means wisdom—a specific, practical excellence and the skill of living by God's design. It is the technical expertise of the soul. For the retiree, it beautifully marks a promotion from professional expert to expert in the Spirit.

The Noon Anchor

The world is saturated with information but starving for Sophia. As a professional, your value was measured by mastery of data and strategic insights. In retirement, this knowledge may feel obsolete, causing profound intellectual displacement. Yet, a Matriarch knows divine wisdom isn't gathered from textbooks; it is beautifully forged over decades. This holy expertise helps you find peace in a quiet house and offer weighty words to a noisy generation. Trade earthly information for His divine insight. Apply your lifetime's craftsmanship to the high-stakes work of spiritual legacy. Ask the Father for His wisdom today.

Reflection Questions

01 Where has your "professional knowledge" reached its limit, leaving you in need of divine Sophia?

02 How does wisdom as a "skill of living" change how you view your daily, hidden choices in retirement?

03 What "raw material" of your past (failure, success, grief) is God asking you to shape into a lesson?

Next Steps

The Skill Inquiry: Identify one difficult relational or personal situation you are facing. Instead of offering a "data-driven" opinion, pray specifically for Sophia and wait for a "skillful" response from the Spirit.

The Wisdom Transfer: Think of one practical "skill for living" you have mastered through your faith (e.g., how to wait well, how to pray through anxiety). Share this expertise with a younger person this week.

Heavenly Father, I thank You that You are the generous source of all wisdom. Forgive me for relying on my own professional knowledge and for neglecting the skill of godly living. I ask for Sophia today. Teach me to take the raw materials of my life and shape them into something that reflects Your glory. Grant me the expertise I need to navigate this season with grace and truth. Amen.

34

THE THEOLOGY OF THE AGING BODY

> For we know that when this earthly tent we live in is taken down (that is, when we die and leave this earthly body), we will have a house in heaven, an eternal body made for us by God himself and not by human hands.
>
> — *2 Corinthians 5:1 (NLT)*

 **The Morning Anchor**

The Greek word *skenos* means a temporary tent or tabernacle. Prone to wear, it was never a permanent home. Calling our body a skenos beautifully signals to the Matriarch that our true, eternal housing is securely waiting for us elsewhere.

 **The Noon Anchor**

Your body is a skenos, a temporary tent slowly folding up. For the professional woman who relied heavily on physical stamina, this natural thinning of tent walls can falsely feel like a catastrophic failure. Yet, biblical theology beautifully reframes this profound decline. These physical limitations are not God's abandonment, but a purposeful relocation of your focus. As the earthly tent becomes fragile, the eternal house becomes more real. Stop patching the tent with frantic desperation to hide your aches. You are a holy pilgrim, Matriarch. Your magnificent, permanent house in heaven is under divine construction.

Reflection Questions

01 How has the relationship with your body changed? Where do you feel "resentment" toward your tent?

02 How do you see the "eternal light" shining through the "thinned walls" of your physical limitations?

03 How does the promise of an "eternal body made by God" change how you view physical decline today?

Next Steps

☐ **The Tent Blessing:** Instead of critiquing your body in the mirror this week, specifically "bless the tent." Thank God for the decades of service your body has provided and acknowledge its temporary holiness.

☐ **The Eternal Focus:** Spend ten minutes each day specifically reflecting on the "house in heaven." Imagine a version of yourself that is no longer subject to the wear and tear of the skenos.

Heavenly Father, I thank You for the earthly tent You have given me to inhabit. Forgive me for my resentment of its limits and my fear of its decline. Help me to treat my body with grace and to recognize its temporary status. Redirect my gaze from this folding tabernacle to the eternal house You have prepared for me. Amen.

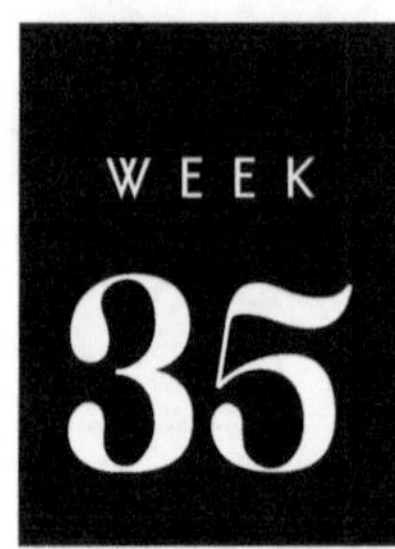

35

RADICAL TRUST VS. SELF-RELIANCE

> 
>
> Trust in the Lord with all your heart; do not depend on your own understanding. Seek his will in all you do, and he will show you which path to take.
>
> — *Proverbs 3:5-6 (NLT)*

 ## The Morning Anchor 

The Hebrew word *batach* means trust, painting a beautiful image of lying face down in total surrender. It requires the intentional collapse of worldly, self-assured confidence. For the retired professional, it means deferring your limited understanding to the divine Architect.

 ## The Noon Anchor

The professional world rewards self-reliance, teaching you that depending completely on yourself ensures absolute security. This deeply ingrained framework often feels like a spiritual virtue, yet in God's Kingdom, it becomes pride preventing radical intimacy. Retirement beautifully removes your paycheck and title so you can finally practice batach. This radical trust is an active choice to stop leaning on your earthly competence. The Matriarch knows her understanding is merely a flickering candle compared to God's brilliant sun. Confront your inner self-made woman. You only need the trust of a child, not a rigid five-year plan.

Reflection Questions

01 In what specific area are you "leaning on your own understanding" instead of God's will?

02 How has professional success made it harder for you to practice the total surrender of batach?

03 What would it look like for you to "lie face down" in trust regarding a worry you currently hold?

Next Steps

The Understanding Fast: Identify one problem you are currently trying to "solve" through worry. Stop thinking about it for twenty-four hours and replace every anxious thought with "I trust You, Father."

The Path Prayer: Before making even a small decision this week, pause and ask, "Father, what is Your will for this moment?" Practice the discipline of asking before acting.

Heavenly Father, I confess that I have lived much of my life relying on my own understanding. Forgive me for my pride and my attempts to be my own provider. I choose to trust You today with all my heart. Teach me the peace of batach. Show me the path You have prepared for me, and help me to walk in it with a quiet spirit. Amen.

INTELLECTUAL LEGACY

> Guard the precious trust which has been committed to you by the Holy Spirit who dwells within us.
>
> *— 2 Timothy 1:14 (NLT)*

The Morning Anchor

The Greek word *paratheke* beautifully means a precious trust or good deposit safely placed with a trusted steward for safekeeping. For the retiree, it represents the profound intellectual and spiritual capital accumulated over a lifetime, a holy deposit you are faithfully guarding.

The Noon Anchor

Most view legacy as distributing physical assets through a will. Yet for the Matriarch, your most significant paratheke is your intellectual and spiritual wealth. You have navigated complex moral dilemmas and survived trials that would crush others. This hard-won wisdom is a good deposit placed within you for the Kingdom. If you retire your mind, you essentially bury your talent. You have a beautiful responsibility to generously pass on your road-tested faith. The next generation is starving for your perspective. Share the profound treasure in your house, Matriarch. Do not let it die with you.

01 What "precious trust" of wisdom or truth has God committed to your care over the last forty years?

02 Are you "burying" your intellectual capital, believing the lie that no one wants to hear an older woman?

03 Who in your circle (a grandchild or neighbor) is spiritually "poor" and needs your stored wisdom?

Next Steps

The Wisdom Inventory: List five "unshakeable truths" you have learned about God through your professional and personal life. Consider how you might "deposit" these into a younger person this month.

The Mentoring Prayer: Ask God to identify one person to whom you can begin passing on your paratheke. Commit to one intentional conversation with them this week.

Heavenly Father, I thank You for the "good deposit" of wisdom You have placed in my life. Forgive me for the times I have hoarded my experiences or doubted their value to others. Help me to be a faithful steward of the truths I have learned. Show me how to pass on my intellectual legacy with grace and humility. Let Your Spirit guard the truth within me. Amen.

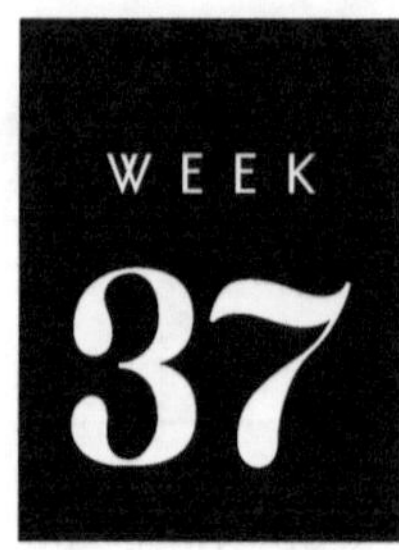

THE GIFT OF SILENCE

> *And after the fire there was the sound of a gentle whisper.*
>
> — *1 Kings 19:12 (NLT)*

The Morning Anchor

The Hebrew word *demamah* means a gentle whisper or calm hush remaining after a great disturbance. It is the beautiful antithesis of professional life's fire and earthquake. For the retiree, silence isn't purposeless; it's the holy laboratory where God becomes audible.

The Noon Anchor

For decades, your career was defined by the roaring fire of urgent demands and the constant earthquake of professional change. In retirement, this relentless social noise finally fades. Many women find this sudden, unstructured silence a deep affliction, feeling utterly invisible without a daily crisis to manage. They quickly escape the hush with endless digital chatter. Yet, for the Kingdom Matriarch, this silence is a divine gift. In this quiet demamah, you confront your singular, unhurried relationship with the Father. Stop performing; practice an undivided gaze. Holy silence develops the internal spiritual weight needed to remain beautifully stable. Be still with God, or remain a fragment endlessly searching the noisy crowd.

Reflection Questions

01 When entering a quiet room, what is your first instinct, and what does it reveal about God's demamah?

02 How has the "noise" of your former career prevented you from hearing God's gentle whisper?

03 In what ways can you transform your current silence into a "holy sanctuary" rather than an "empty void"?

Next Steps

☐ **The Whisper Practice:** Set a timer for twenty minutes this week. Sit in absolute silence with no distractions, no music, and no books. Practice being "undivided" and listening for the demamah.

☐ **The Noise Fast:** Instead of automatically calling someone or turning on the news when the house feels "too quiet," spend ten minutes specifically asking God to whisper His peace to your soul.

Heavenly Father, I thank You for the gift of silence. Forgive me for my fear of the quiet and my attempt to escape Your gentle whisper with the noise of the world. I choose the "better part" today. Help me to find my wholeness in Your presence alone. Let my silence be a place of consultation rather than a place of dread. Amen.

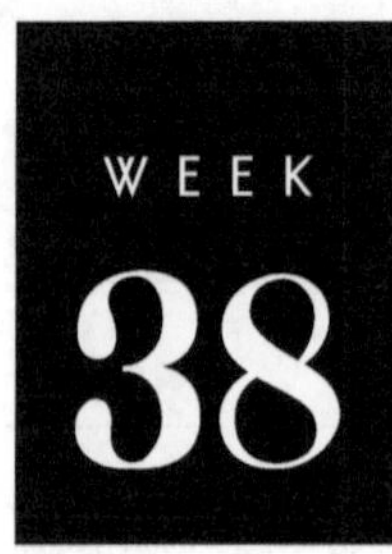

38

THE DISCIPLINED MIND

> 66
>
> For God has not given us a spirit of fear and timidity, but of power, love, and self-discipline.
>
> — *2 Timothy 1:7 (NLT)*
>
> 99

 **The Morning Anchor** ···

The Greek word *sophronismos* means mental discipline or a sound mind. It describes being stable, balanced, and beautifully controlled. In antiquity, it defined leaders remaining calm during crisis. For the retiree, it is the essential discipline keeping your intellect sharp.

 **The Noon Anchor** ···

When you worked, your mind was beautifully disciplined by external career demands. Without that pressure, you risk mental drift, letting your intellect go soft. Consumed by trivialities or cultural fear, your thoughts lose focus. A Matriarch knows mental health requires rigorous spiritual discipline. God gave you a spirit of power and love, mediated through a sound mind. Guard your thoughts against the heavy fog of late life apathy by maintaining a rich intellect. Reject passive media consumption; claim your sophronismos. You are not losing your edge, Matriarch; you are intentionally honing it for the Kingdom.

Reflection Questions

01 In what areas of your life is the "spirit of fear or timidity" currently clouding your judgment or your peace?

02 How have you allowed your mind to go "soft" in retirement? What "intellectual weight" must you lift?

03 What would a "sound mind" (sophronismos) look like during current family or personal challenges?

Next Steps

The Mental Filter: Audit your media consumption for one day. Identify anything that produces "fear or timidity" rather than "power and love." Disconnect from at least one source of mental noise.

The Intellectual Exercise: Choose one difficult chapter of scripture or a theological concept and commit to "memorizing the logic" of it this week. Force your mind to be disciplined and focused.

Heavenly Father, I thank You for the spirit of power, love, and self-discipline You have given me. Forgive me for my mental laziness and my surrender to fear. I claim the gift of sophronismos today. Help me to keep my mind sharp and my spirit focused on Your truth. Let my thoughts be governed by Your Spirit so that I may walk in Your power. Amen.

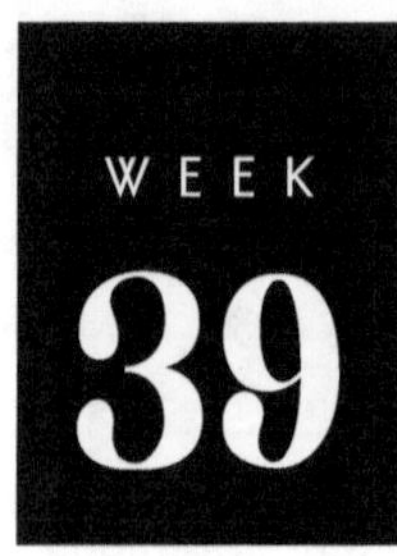

39

REVIEW OF THE MIND

> Fix your thoughts on what is true, and honorable, and right, and pure, and lovely, and admirable. Think about things that are excellent and worthy of praise.
>
> — *Philippians 4:8 (NLT)*

The Morning Anchor

The Greek word *logizomai* means to deliberately reckon, calculate, or take a full inventory. This mathematical term requires a systematic mental evaluation. For the retiree, this vital Third Quarter Review beautifully checks if your intellectual house holds God's excellent things.

The Noon Anchor

You have completed the third section of your journey, focusing on deep mental renovation. This week is your Third Quarter Review. Be an accountant of the intellect, deliberately evaluating your thoughts. Are you becoming a woman whose mind is a cathedral of truth, or merely a warehouse of worldly anxieties? If we fix our thoughts on fading things, we feel empty. Fixing them on what is true and honorable brings peace. This is the beautiful fruit of logizomai. Take your intellectual inventory with profound gratitude, Matriarch. You are fully ready for the final quarter.

01 Taking inventory of your thoughts today, what percentage is occupied by things "worthy of praise"?

02 How has your mind's "renovation" over thirteen weeks changed how you handle family or health stress?

03 Which theological concept here has become the most "stable" and "true" anchor for your intellect?

Next Steps

☐ **The Mental Inventory:** Write down the five most frequent thoughts you have had this week. Evaluate them against the list in Philippians 4:8. If they are not "excellent," replace them with a specific praise.

☐ **The Section Audit:** Reread your journaling prompts from Week 27 through Week 38. Identify the most significant shift in your "intellectual house" and thank God for the renovation.

Heavenly Father, I thank You for the renewal of my mind. Forgive me for the "excellent" things I have ignored and the "trivial" things I have obsessed over. Help me to be a faithful accountant of my thoughts. Fix my mind on what is true, honorable, and pure. Let my intellect be a cathedral that honors Your name. Amen.

Congratulations, Matriarch. You have completed the most intellectually rigorous section of your Year of Refirement. This section was designed to move you from professional knowledge to divine wisdom and to renovate your mental architecture for the Kingdom. Before we move into Section 4, pause here to evaluate the weight of your current theology.

Reflection Questions

01 How does the title "Ancient of Days" shift your perspective on aging and your perceived invisibility?

02 In what ways has the "Digital Sabbath" or the "Gift of Silence" restored the hesychia (quietness) of your soul?

03 What specific part of theology (Suffering, The Body, or Metanoia) has been the most difficult for you to process, and what fruit has it produced in your character?

The Intellectual Stewardship: Identify one "good deposit" of wisdom you have gained in this section and share it with a younger woman this week. Be intentional about passing on the substance of the Word.

The Rule Update: Review your "Rule of Life" from Week 11. Does it include enough intellectual weight (study, silence, or reflection) to sustain your renewed mind?

The Great Bridge: From Ceasing to Commission

Entering our final quarter, we resolve a beautiful paradox: ceasing the professional grind not for dormancy, but a Kingdom commission. Advancing to legacy, holy silence trades worldly expertise for the Matriarch's divine authority.

Heavenly Father, we thank You for the substance of Your Word. You have challenged our minds and renovated our thinking. Forgive us for our intellectual laziness and our fear of the deep. As we move into the final quarter of our year, let the wisdom we have gathered become the foundation of our legacy. Keep our minds sharp, our hearts whole, and our gaze fixed on Your unshakeable Kingdom. We trust Your craftsmanship. Amen.

04

THE LITURGY OF
THE ENCORE

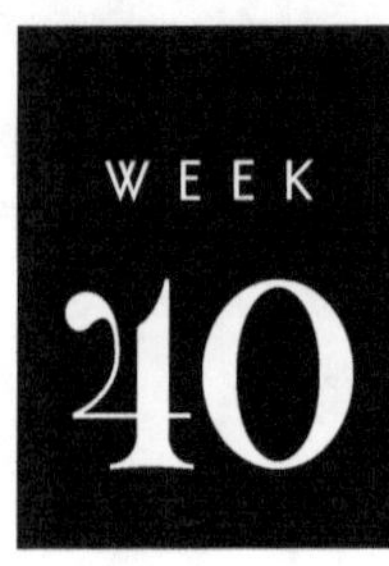

40

THE COMMUTE TO THE THRONE

> Let me hear of your unfailing love each morning, for I am trusting you. Show me where to walk, for I give myself to you.
>
> — *Psalm 143:8 (NLT)*

The Morning Anchor

The Hebrew word *boqer* means morning, rooted in breaking forth or inquiring. More than a time of day, it is a spiritual threshold. For the retiree, boqer beautifully replaces your professional commute, becoming an intentional threshold to inquire of the Lord.

The Noon Anchor

During your long career, mornings were a frantic race to prove your worth through speed and constant problem solving. In retirement, this ingrained urgency often remains, causing spiritual disorientation if spent on worldly distractions rather than Kingdom news. A wise Matriarch beautifully redirects this discipline. The end of your earthly commute begins your holy commute to the throne. Apply your former professional concentration to seeking the Creator. Reclaim the boqer. Stop rushing into the digital void; intentionally linger at the heavenly throne. Ask the Father where to walk, beautifully fueled by His unfailing love instead of exhausting daily work deadlines.

01   What is the first thing that "breaks forth" in your mind upon waking, and how does it shape your peace?

02   How can you use the discipline of your former commute to create a new, holy threshold each morning?

03   In what specific area of your life right now are you most in need of God "showing you where to walk" today?

Next Steps

☐ **The Throne Threshold:** Designate a specific chair or a space in your home as your "Throne Room." For seven days, do not check your phone or turn on the news until you have spent fifteen minutes at this threshold.

☐ **The Inquiry Prayer:** Before you get out of bed, pray the words of Psalm 143:8. Specifically ask God to "show you where to walk" in the quiet hours of your Tuesday.

Heavenly Father, I thank You for the breaking of the light this morning. Forgive me for the times I have rushed into the day without seeking Your face. I choose to make my first commute to Your throne. Show me where to walk and let me hear of Your unfailing love. Help me to find my direction in Your Spirit rather than the demands of the world. Amen.

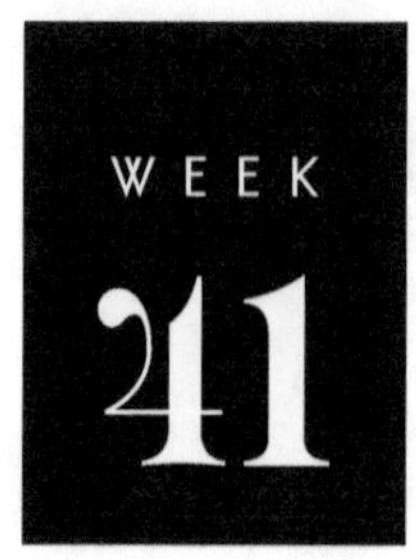

ZAQEN: THE WEIGHT OF GLORY

> And now, O Lord, you have made me king instead of my father, David, but I am like a little child who doesn't know his way around. And here I am in the midst of your own chosen people, a nation so great and numerous they cannot be counted! Give me an understanding heart so that I can govern your people well and know the difference between right and wrong. For who by himself is able to govern this great people of yours?
>
> — *1 Kings 3:7-9 (NLT)*

 **The Morning Anchor**

The Hebrew word *zaqen* refers to an elder, while kabod means weight or glory. In the Matriarch, these beautifully link: the silver hair of the zaqen is the outward sign of inward kabod. You aren't merely aging; you are becoming substantial.

 **The Noon Anchor**

In retirement, you profoundly shift from professional expert to a community zaqen. Formerly valued for technical utility, you are now valued for immense spiritual weight. Modern culture has older citizens but few true elders, as many shed responsibilities for passive leisure. Yet, a Matriarch's gray hair is her divine commission. You carry a stabilizing kabod, a beautiful thickness of soul forged through decades of faithful devotion. Stop apologizing for your age. You are a living repository of glory, holy Matriarch.

01 Do you currently view your age as a "weight" of glory or as a "burden" of physical decline?

02 How do you distinguish a "senior" consuming leisure from a zaqen carrying stabilizing kabod?

03 Who in your life right now needs the understanding heart and discerning weight you've gained?

Next Steps

☐ **The Weighty Word:** Identify one younger person who is currently facing a "right or wrong" dilemma. Offer them a word of discernment, not as a casual opinion, but as a weight of wisdom from your walk with God.

☐ **The Solomon Prayer:** Spend ten minutes this week specifically praying Solomon's prayer for an understanding heart. Ask God to show you how to govern your current relational influence with kabod.

Heavenly Father, I thank You for the weight of the years You have given me. Forgive me for wanting to be "light" and "carefree" when You have called me to be an elder. Give me an understanding heart so that I may discern Your truth in a confused world. Help me to use my wisdom to stabilize those around me and to lead with the dignity of a Zaqen. Amen.

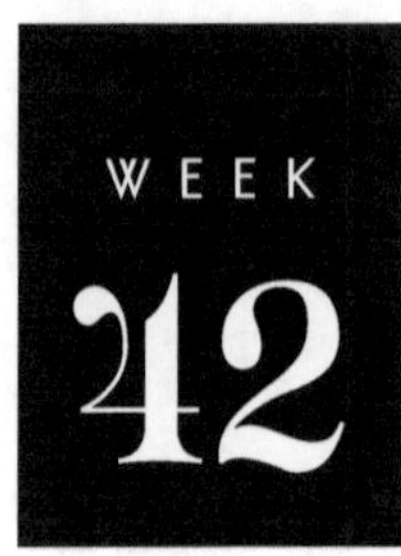

42

THE NOON ANCHOR

> It is good to give thanks to the Lord, to sing praises to the Most High. It is good to proclaim your unfailing love in the morning and your faithfulness every evening.
>
> — *Psalm 92:1-2 (NLT)*

 **The Morning Anchor**

The Hebrew word *emunah* means faithfulness, referring to absolute firmness, stability, and reliability like a strong pillar. While morning brings unfailing love and evening brings testimony, emunah bridges them. For the retiree, the Noon Anchor intentionally reconnects these beautiful truths.

 **The Noon Anchor**

During your career, noon was structured by productivity. In retirement, this unstructured middle is dangerous, where digital noise and aimless drift are pervasive. Without a deliberate anchor, morning peace is lost in the muddle. The Noon Anchor is your vital spiritual recalibration. By pausing to praise God, you refuse accidental moments, beautifully consecrating your entire day. This midday pause creates the emunah of your retirement, ensuring you redeem time rather than merely pass it. Proclaim His faithfulness during your unstructured Tuesday. Stability requires a centered soul, not a busy schedule. Keep the anchor deep, Matriarch.

Reflection Questions

01 How does a midday "Noon Anchor" change how you handle the "unstructured drift" of your afternoons?

02 In what specific moments of your day do you feel your soul beginning to "totter" or lose its stability?

03 How does proclaiming God's emunah (faithfulness) at noon change your evening prayer reflections?

Next Steps

The Midday Pause: For seven days, set an alarm for exactly 12:00 PM. Stop whatever you are doing and spend five minutes simply proclaiming the emunah of God over your home and your family.

The Song of Praise: Find one hymn or song of praise that specifically focuses on God's faithfulness. Play it or sing it during your Noon Anchor this week to "sing praises to the Most High."

Heavenly Father, I thank You for Your unfailing love in the morning and Your faithfulness every evening. Forgive me for the times I have allowed the middle of my day to drift into distraction or apathy. I choose to anchor my soul in You today. Be the pillar of stability in my house. Help me to proclaim Your faithfulness even in the quietest hours of my afternoon. Amen.

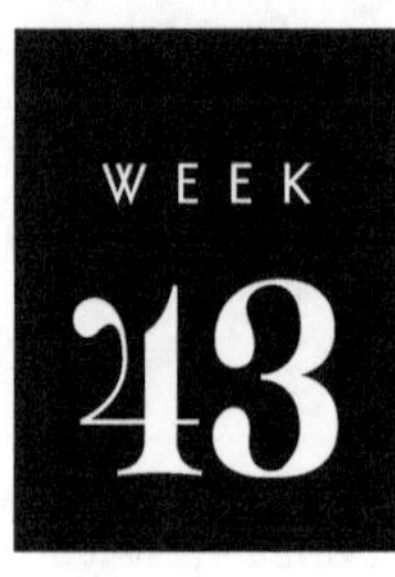

THE EXAMEN OF PURPOSE

> May the Lord our God be with us as he was with our ancestors; may he never abandon us or leave us. May he give us the desire to do his will in everything we do and to walk in all his ways and obey the commands, decrees, and regulations that he gave our ancestors.
>
> — *1 Kings 8:57-58 (NLT)*

 **The Morning Anchor**

The Hebrew word *natah* means to stretch out, spread, or bend. It describes a deliberate leaning of your will toward God. Because our hearts naturally drift, they must be intentionally bent back. The Examen beautifully checks this daily holy bend.

 **The Noon Anchor**

As a professional, you relied on regular performance reviews to ensure alignment with organizational goals. In retirement, without a boss, your review becomes an internal, spiritual Examen of Purpose. A Matriarch doesn't measure daily productivity; she reviews how her heart was inclined toward the Father. Did you gracefully obey Him in hidden moments? This isn't self-condemnation, but holy alignment. We often bend away through distraction or fear. The Examen beautifully allows you to bend back toward God before sleep, ensuring an intentional walk of obedience. Measure your day by its natah. Adjust the bend, Matriarch.

Reflection Questions

01 Looking back today, does your heart "lean" more toward worldly anxiety or the ways of God?

02 What scriptural "command or decree" was hardest for you to obey in today's unstructured quiet?

03 How does God's promise to "never abandon us" change how you face failures in your nightly review?

Next Steps

The Nightly Review: For five minutes before bed, review your day in reverse. Identify one moment where you "bent" toward God and one moment where you "bent" toward yourself. Ask for the natah of the Spirit for tomorrow.

The Ancestor Focus: Think of one godly woman from your family history. Ask God to help you "walk in her ways" of faithfulness as you obey the commands He has given you.

Heavenly Father, I thank You that You are with me as You were with those who came before me. Forgive me for the times my heart has bent away from Your will today. I ask You to incline my heart toward Your ways tonight. Teach me to walk in Your paths and to obey Your commands with a joyful spirit. May I never feel abandoned, for I am Your child. Amen.

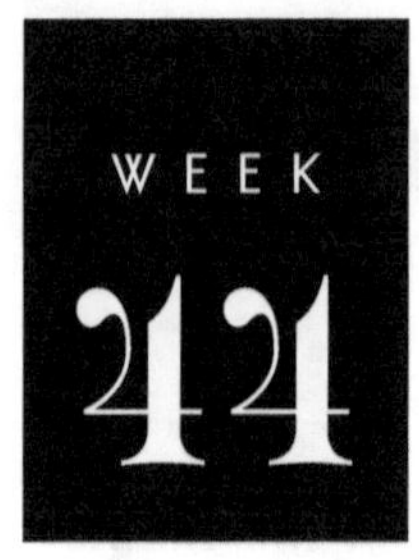

MENTORING THE NEXT GENERATION

> Similarly, teach the older women to live in a way that honors God. They must not slander others or be heavy drinkers. Instead, they should teach others what is good. These older women must train the younger women to love their husbands and their children.
>
> — *Titus 2:3-4 (NLT)*

 **The Morning Anchor**

The Greek word *sophronizo* means to train, gently bringing someone to their senses through self-control. It is not academic instruction, but beautiful relational tuning. For the retiree, it profoundly transitions you from managing employees to intentionally training the younger hearts.

 **The Noon Anchor**

In your career, you managed processes and mentored colleagues for organizational productivity. In retirement, however, you are beautifully called to be a spiritual mother. Many shy away, fearing they lack modern relevance, confusing technological knowledge with spiritual wisdom. Yet, younger women do not need spreadsheet help; they need deep soul help. Fragmented by familiar professional pressures, they need you to intentionally sophronizo them. You are not a boss; you are a trellis, helping younger vines grow. Your lifelong expertise is a holy deposit. Offer fainting women a seat, Matriarch. You are the theologian in residence.

Reflection Questions

01 Why do you feel hesitation or "imposter syndrome" mentoring younger women in your community?

02 Where has God "brought you to your senses," and how can you share this without being patronizing?

03 Who is the "younger woman" in your circle right now who seems the most "fragmented" by life's demands?

Next Steps

☐ **The Mentoring Invitation:** Identify one younger woman and invite her for coffee or tea this week. Instead of offering advice, ask her, "What is the hardest thing you are navigating right now?" and listen with an "elder's heart."

☐ **The Sophronizo Prayer:** Specifically pray for the "self-control and moderation" of the younger women in your family or church. Ask God to show you how to be a trellis for their growth.

Heavenly Father, I thank You for the wisdom You have accumulated in me through the years. Forgive me for my fear of being "overbearing" and for my hesitation to share Your truth. Help me to be a faithful mentor to the younger generation. Teach me to sophronizo those around me with grace and humility. Let my life be a trellis that supports the growth of others for Your glory. Amen.

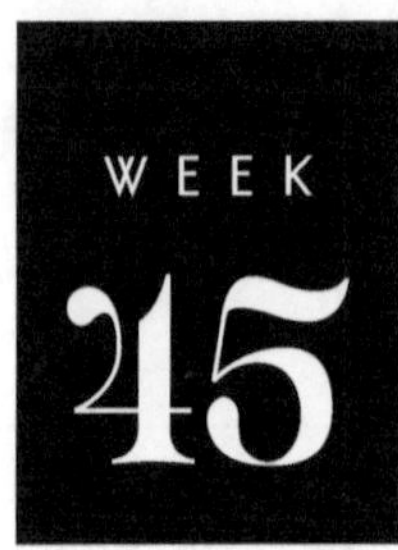

45

THE ENCORE CAREER

> Even in old age they will still produce fruit; they will remain vital and green. They will declare, The Lord is just! He is my rock! There is no injustice in him!
>
> — *Psalm 92:14-15 (NLT)*

The Morning Anchor

The Hebrew word *nub* beautifully means to produce fruit, flourish, or sprout persistently. Unlike a fading seasonal bloom, it suggests divine vitality independent of physical youth. For the retiree, it truly pictures an Encore Career of ongoing, vibrant spiritual productivity.

The Noon Anchor

This world views retirement as your career's completion, expecting you to step offstage. Yet, the Bible views aging as a season of persistent flourishing. You are called to an Encore Career for the Kingdom. Your forty years of strategic thinking and deep empathy were not meant to be retired, but beautifully refired for a new mission. Shift from professional ambition to Kingdom vitality, intentionally deploying skills for a cause that outlives you. You are not formerly employed; you are divinely commissioned. Look at your toolbox with fresh eyes today. The stage is still yours, Matriarch.

Reflection Questions

01 If you were to rebrand your career expertise for the Kingdom, what would be your new "job description"?

02 In what areas of your life right now do you feel "dry and brown" rather than "vital and green," and why?

03 What one "fruit" of your character do you want to produce most intensely in your Encore years?

Next Steps

☐ **The Toolbox Audit:** List three professional skills you mastered in your career. Identify one Kingdom-focused way you could "deploy" each skill this month.

☐ **The Flourishing Prayer:** Ask God to show you the "Encore mission" He has specifically designed for your unique set of experiences and talents. Commit to one small step toward that mission this week.

Heavenly Father, I thank You that I am still called to produce fruit even in my later years. Forgive me for my spiritual laziness and my fear of being "finished." I choose to remain vital and green in Your house. Rebrand my skills for Your Kingdom mission. Help me to declare Your justice and Your faithfulness through the work of my hands and the fruit of my heart. Amen.

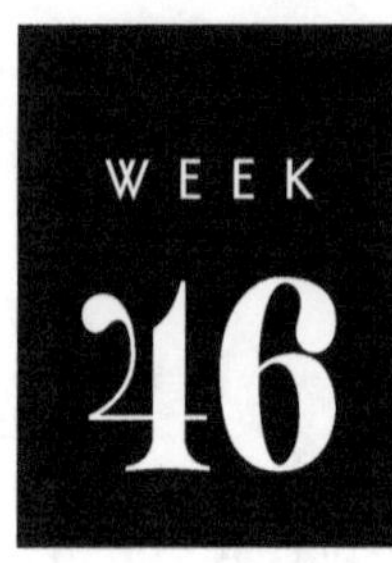

46

TELEIOS: THE RIPENED SOUL

> So don't let your grip slacken. For when your endurance is fully developed, you will be perfect and complete, needing nothing.
>
> —James 1:4 (NLT)

 **The Morning Anchor**

The Greek word *teleios* means perfect or mature, describing something reaching its intended goal or finished state. Like fruit finally ripening on the vine, it isn't moral flawlessness. For the retiree, it beautifully represents the finishing school of the soul.

 **The Noon Anchor**

In your career, you relentlessly pursued horizontal perfection, growing in competitive skills and professional accuracy. God, however, is beautifully interested in your vertical *teleios.* He uses retirement's shaking to fully develop your endurance. You aren't at the end; you are at your glorious consummation.

A ripened soul is perfect, complete, and profoundly needs nothing. This is true ultimate freedom. You no longer need a title or paycheck to feel secure. You are becoming the fully ripened masterpiece God intentionally designed. Embrace the Spirit's finishing work. Maturing toward teleios, you find absolute satisfaction in Him, Matriarch.

Reflection Questions

01 In what area are you still feeling "incomplete," needing something from the world to feel whole?

02 How has the shaking of your retirement actually helped you reach a higher level of teleios or spiritual ripening?

03 What does biblical "perfect and complete" look like for a woman of your age and experience?

Next Steps

The Ripening Check: Identify one worldly thing you think you need to be happy. Practice the discipline of "needing nothing" by surrendering that thing to God for twentyfour hours.

The Maturity Focus: Choose one trait of spiritual maturity, such as patience or humility, and consciously focus on that "fruit" this week, asking God to complete His ripening work in you.

Heavenly Father, I thank You that You are bringing my soul to its intended goal. Forgive me for my desire for worldly perfection and my impatience with Your process of ripening. I choose to let my endurance be fully developed. Make me teleios: perfect and complete, needing nothing but Your presence. Amen.

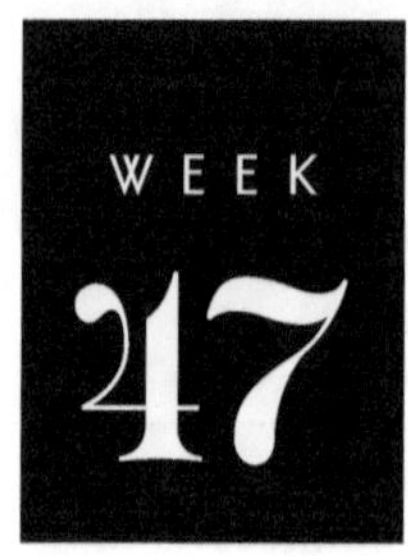

APOSTELLŌ: THE SENT LEGACY

> Never be lazy, but work hard and serve the Lord enthusiastically. Rejoice in our confident hope. Be patient in trouble, and keep on praying.
>
> — *Romans 12:11-12 (NLT)*

The Morning Anchor

The Greek word *apostellō* means a holy commission, sent forth with a specific mission and the sender's full authority. For the retiree, this beautifully reveals your Third Act is not a retreat, but a divine deployment into the next generation.

The Noon Anchor

In your career, you managed projects under organizational authority. Finishing that professional race, you may falsely feel your commissioning has ended. Yet, a Matriarch knows ending this race begins her glorious Kingdom deployment.

You are being beautifully *apostellō* into your community with a specific, holy commission. You are not finished; you are relocated. You carry the profound authority of a finished race into every conversation. You are an authorized witness of God's faithfulness. Your history earns you the right to be sent with truth. Do not stay put spiritually, Matriarch. Deliver your sacred wisdom today.

01 If you are "sent with authority" rather than "retired," how does your posture toward family change?

02 What specific "deposit of truth" do you feel most commissioned to deliver to the next generation?

03 Where are you staying put spiritually when God asks you to be apostellō into a new area of service?

Next Steps

☐ **The Commission Statement:** Write out a one-sentence "Apostolic Commission" for your current week. Who are you sent to, and what truth are you sent to deliver?

☐ **The Authority Practice:** In your next interaction with a younger person, consciously speak from the authority of your finished race. Offer a word that is sent by the Spirit rather than a casual opinion.

Heavenly Father, I thank You that You are still the One who sends me. Forgive me for my desire to retreat and my fear that my commission has ended. I choose to be apostellō today. Help me to carry the authority of my faithfulness into the lives of the next generation. Grant me the courage to deliver Your truth with strength and dignity. Amen.

THE FEARLESS FORWARD

> She is clothed with strength and dignity, and she laughs without fear of the future. When she speaks, her words are wise, and she gives instructions with kindness.
>
> — *Proverbs 31:25-26 (NLT)*

The Morning Anchor

The Hebrew word *yare* means fear, ranging from dread to holy awe. The Proverbs woman laughing without yare isn't naive; she operates from radical security. For the retiree, it beautifully transitions you from calculating earthly risks to celebrating God's sovereignty.

The Noon Anchor

As a professional, you relentlessly anticipated problems and mitigated risks. In retirement, this anticipatory anxiety often turns inward toward health and finances, causing you to shrink back into safe, small movements. Yet, a Matriarch is beautifully clothed with divine strength and dignity. Clothed by the Father, your posture shifts from dread to a fearless laugh. This theological statement boldly declares the world's "what ifs" are no match for God's "I am." Stop trying to control the future through worry. You are not fading into fearful old age; you are walking forward into fearless legacy, Matriarch.

Reflection Questions

01 What specific "what if" regarding your future currently causes you the most "dread" or "shrinking back"?

02 How would your daily posture change if you truly felt "clothed with strength and dignity" by the Father?

03 How can your "fearless forward" laugh be a testimony to a younger generation terrified of aging?

Next Steps

The Fear Exchange: Write down your primary fear for the next five years. Physically place it in your Bible at Proverbs 31 and consciously "clothe" that fear in God's strength.

The Instruction of Kindness: Identify a situation this week where you would normally be "anxious or controlling." Intentionally offer a "wise instruction given with kindness" instead.

Heavenly Father, I thank You that You clothe me with strength and dignity. Forgive me for my dread of the future and my attempt to manage the unknown through worry. I choose to laugh without fear today. Help me to walk forward with a holy awe of Your sovereignty. Let my words be wise and my heart be kind as I trust in Your perfect care. Amen.

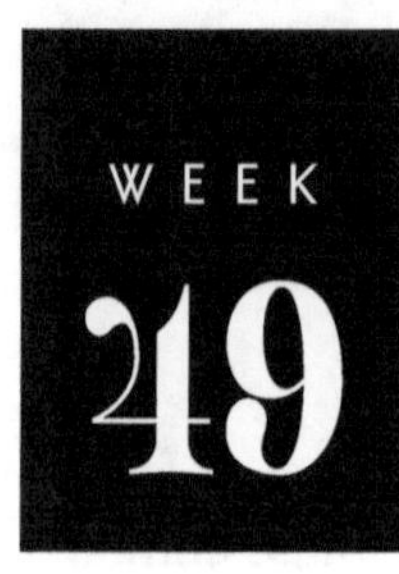

49

THE STEWARDSHIP OF INFLUENCE

> For God is at work within you, helping you want to obey him and then helping you do what he pleases. Do everything without complaining and arguing, so that no one can criticize you. Live clean, innocent lives as children of God, shining like bright lights in a world full of crooked and perverse people.
>
> — *Philippians 2:13-15 (NLT)*

 **The Morning Anchor**

The Greek word *phaino* means shining or appearing, purposefully bringing light into dark spaces to reveal reality. It is a steady, radiant influence. For the retiree, this beautifully stewards your Third Act voice, illuminating God's truth through your holy character.

 **The Noon Anchor**

In your career, influence was positional. People listened because of your title. In retirement, personal influence begins. Many equate losing their title with losing their voice. Yet, a Matriarch knows her influence is now a stewardship of light. You are called to phaino, shining brightly in a crooked world. People are still watching how you handle aging and treat the vulnerable. Your clean, innocent life is more powerful than any professional directive you ever issued. Stop mourning lost professional power and start managing your spiritual light. You are a lighthouse, Matriarch. Steward your radiant light.

121

Reflection Questions

01 Where is the "world's noise" loudest in your family or community, and how can you *phaino* (shine) there?

02 How has your "voice" changed post-career? Are you using it to "complain" or "reveal the light"?

03 What is one specific way you can "do what pleases God" this week to serve as a bright light to others?

Next Steps

☐ **The Complaint Fast:** For three days this week, commit to doing everything without "complaining or arguing." Observe how this silence creates a "space for light" in your interactions.

☐ **The Influence Audit:** Identify one social or community circle where you have influence. Ask God to show you one "radiant" truth you can speak into that circle this week.

Heavenly Father, I thank You that You are at work within me. Forgive me for hiding my light and for joining in the complaining of the world. I choose to steward my influence for Your glory today. Help me to live a clean and innocent life so that I may shine like a bright light. Let my voice reveal Your truth and Your peace to those who are lost in the dark. Amen.

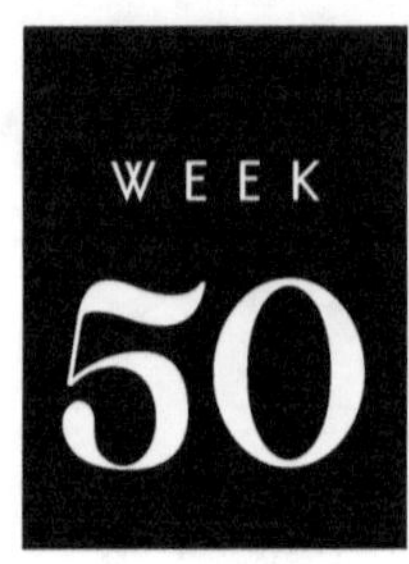

50

THE ETERNAL PERSPECTIVE

> Look! I am making everything new!
>
> — *Revelation 21:5 (NLT)*

The Morning Anchor

The Greek word *kainos* means new in nature or refreshed, rather than chronological time. It describes a radical transformation superseding the old. For the retiree preoccupied with physical decline, this beautifully promises our final arrival is being made entirely new

The Noon Anchor

Approaching your first retirement anniversary, you likely feel deep bodily weariness and shaken worldly securities. Our modern culture relentlessly markets a carefree "Golden Age," yet reality often feels like being painfully unclothed, losing jobs, daily stamina, and cherished loved ones. Focusing only on this earthly decay causes profound spiritual mourning. However, a wise Matriarch intentionally looks toward the eternal New City. You are not just being taken apart by time; you are being purposefully made new. Your physical limitations and hidden griefs are merely raw materials for the beautiful *kainos* that God is bringing forth. You are not finishing a life, Matriarch; you are beginning a glorious, unending spiritual transformation.

01 How do you focus on the "old" (career, fading stamina) instead of the life (kainos) God is building?

02 How does God's promise to make all things new reshape your view of physical or emotional decline?

03 What would it look like to live this week with an "Eternal Perspective" of God's Kingdom?

Next Steps

The New Focus: Spend fifteen minutes this week reading Revelation 21 and 22. Specifically focus on the phrase "making everything new" and apply it to one specific area of your current life.

The *Kainos* Declaration: Every time you feel "old or tired" this week, speak the word kainos as a reminder that your true identity is being refreshed and transformed by God.

Heavenly Father, I thank You that You are making everything new. Forgive me for my obsession with the old and my fear of the decay of my current life. I choose to live with an eternal perspective today. Help me to long for the kainos quality of Your Kingdom and to find my peace in the promise of Your restoration. I trust Your fresh work in me. Amen.

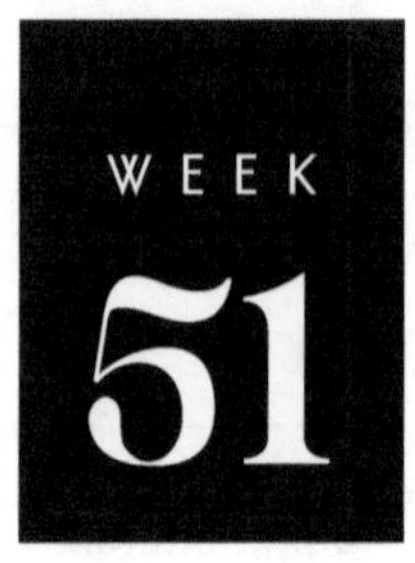

TODAH : THE THANKSGIVING SACRIFICE

> Give thanks to the Lord, for he is good! His faithful love endures forever. Has the Lord redeemed you? Then speak out! Tell others he has redeemed you from your enemies.
>
> — Psalm 107:1-2 (NLT)

 **The Morning Anchor**

The Hebrew word *todah* means thanksgiving, a specific Temple sacrifice offering public proclamation of rescue from profound danger. For the retiree, todah is the vocal declaration that God has beautifully delivered your soul from the dark prison of professional idolatry.

 **The Noon Anchor**

You have reached the final weeks of a year marked by radical transition. Initially, retirement perhaps felt like imprisonment or the painful death of professional relevance as you wrestled the heavy Idol of Productivity. Yet, looking back, you see a magnificent history of divine rescue. The Father redeemed you from constantly proving your worth through exhausting labor. Therefore, the Matriarch must offer a todah. This is no polite thank you; it is a powerful, public testimony of deliverance. Speak out your glorious redemption story. Has the Lord fully redeemed you, Matriarch? Then speak out today.

Reflection Questions

01 From what "enemy" (anxiety, status-seeking, bitterness) has God redeemed you in this transition?

02 Why does "speaking out" your redemption feel like a "sacrifice" of your privacy or your professional pride?

03 Who in your life right now is "imprisoned" by the same fears you once had and needs to hear your todah?

Next Steps

☐ **The Proclamation Write-Up:** Draft a short "Redemption Story" from your first year of retirement. Specifically name the "enemy" God rescued you from and the "faithful love" He showed you.

☐ **The Todah Meal:** Invite a friend or a family member to a meal this week. Intentionally "speak out" one specific way the Lord has redeemed your purpose in this season.

Heavenly Father, I thank You that You are my Rescuer. Forgive me for my quietness and my failure to speak of Your redemption. I offer my todah to You today. I thank You for delivering me from the idols of my past and the fears of my future. Let my story of Your faithful love be a sacrifice of praise that encourages others. Amen.

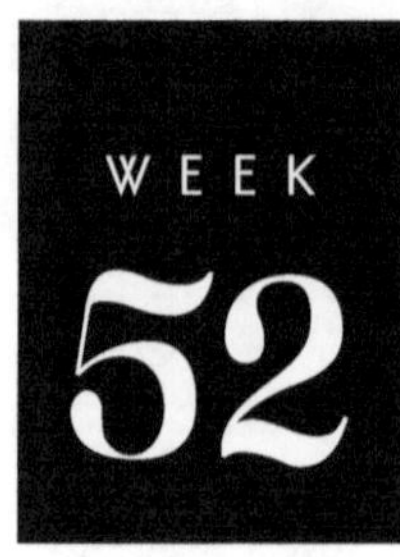

THE COMMISSION

> I have fought the good fight, I have finished the race, and I have remained faithful. And now the prize awaits me—the crown of righteousness, which the Lord, the righteous Judge, will give me on the day of his return. And the prize is not just for me but for all who eagerly look forward to his appearing.
>
> — 2 Timothy 4:7-8 (NLT)

The Morning Anchor

The Hebrew word *shalach* means to send or commission, describing a formal deployment with the sender's full authority. For the retiree, finishing this year is not a finish line but a beautiful deployment into the permanent encore of your life.

The Noon Anchor

You have finished the year, but the race continues. Deconstructing the worker to find the daughter, you are beautifully promoted to the spiritual command center. Having fought a good professional fight, you are now commissioned into the greatest fight for Kingdom legacy. Your Year of Refirement was merely the training ground; today is your divine deployment. Your prize is a glorious crown of righteousness. As a commissioned Elder, guard your precious trust. Stop looking for a finish line; embrace your holy mission field. Step boldly into your permanent encore with divine strength and dignity, Matriarch.

127

01 How has your view of "the finish line" changed after fifty-two weeks of this spiritual journey?

02 What is the specific "good fight" that God is calling you to focus on in the coming year of your retirement?

03 How does the "crown of righteousness" change the way you value your daily, hidden acts of faithfulness today?

Next Steps

☐ **The Final Commission:** Write out your "Matriarch's Commission." Using the word shalach, draft a one-sentence statement of your mission for the next year.

☐ **The Legacy Gift:** Give this book or a similar resource to another woman who is just beginning her "Final Commute." Pass on the commission.

Heavenly Father, I thank You that You have brought me through this "Year of Refirement." Forgive me for wanting to stop when You have called me to go. I accept my commission today as a Matriarch in Your house. Help me to fight the good fight and to remain faithful to the end. I look forward to Your appearing and I trust in the prize You have prepared for me. Amen.

MILESTONE REVIEW

You have successfully completed the final quarter of your year and reached the conclusion of your "Authenticity Compass." This section was designed to move you from the "Deconstruction" of your former life into the "Commission" of your legacy. Before you close this book, pause for a final evaluation of your journey.

Reflection Questions

01 How has the "Commute to the Throne" replaced the "Commute to the Office" as your daily anchor?

02 How has the "Liturgy of Gratitude" reshaped how you see the "Negative Spaces" you navigated this year?

03 What does it mean to be a *Zaqen* in your community, and how will you steward that weight?

☐ **The Rule Permanence:** Take your "Refined Rule of Life" and finalize it as your "Liturgy for the Third Act." Commit to living this rhythm as your permanent spiritual scaffolding.

☐ **The Fearless Walk:** Identify one "new territory" for the Kingdom that you were previously too afraid to enter. Step into it this week as a commissioned Matriarch.

Heavenly Father, we thank You for the year You have given us. You have been our Ebenezer and our Guide. You have deconstructed our idols and crowned us with Your glory. As we go forward as commissioned Matriarchs, stay close to us. Help us to fight the good fight and to remain faithful in every quiet moment. We long for Your appearing and we trust Your righteousness. We are Your children, and we are home. Amen.

APPENDIX

A Guide for the Matriarch's Journey

Use this index to navigate the theological anchors, word studies,and action items of your Year of Refirement.

Aging and Physicality

- *Fearless Forward*: Posture toward the future (Week 48)
- *Gray Hair as a Crown*: The tipharah of wisdom (Week 12)
- *Kainos*: The quality of being made new (Week 50)
- *Skenos*: The theology of the folding tent (Week 34)
- *Stewardship of Energy*: The finite nature of koach (Week 22)
- *Zaqen and Kabod*: The weight of the elder (Week 41)

Boundaries and Relational Health

- *Acaph*: Being held close in family silence (Week 17)
- *Bethany Boundary*: Reclaiming your seat at the feet of Christ (Week 14)
- *Gebul*: Marking the holiness of borders (Week 16)
- *Grandmother Burnout*: The sufficiency of charis (Week 15)
- *Marriage Recalibration*: Learning to walk as a syzygos (Week 20)
- *Relational Legacy*: The shanan of sharpening others (Week 25)
- *Wisdom of "No"*: The radical simplicity of nai and ou (Week 23)

Identity and Purpose

- *Anapausis*: The rest of the final commute (Week 1)
- *Apostellō*: The sent and commissioned legacy (Week 47)
- *Encore Career*: The nub of persistent fruitfulness (Week 45)
- *Kenosis*: The emptying of professional ego (Week 6)
- *Poiema*: Your identity as God's masterpiece (Week 9)
- *Teknon*: Status as a child without a title (Week 3)

Intellectual and Spiritual Growth

- *Ananeoo:* The structural renovation of the mind (Week 29)
- *Atiq Yomin:* Anchoring in the Ancient of Days (Week 27)
- *Faith Shifting:* Navigating the saleuo of doubt (Week 30)
- *Intellectual Hunger:* Pursuing anakainosis (Week 10)
- *Sophia:* The skill of living in the Third Act (Week 33)
- *Sophronismos:* The discipline of a sound mind (Week 38)
- *Teleios:* The ripening and maturity of the soul (Week 46)

Pain and Negative Spaces

- *Dumiyyah:* Silent waiting in solo wholeness (Week 21)
- *El Roi:* The God who sees the invisible woman (Week 19)
- *Financial Anxiety:* Combating merimnao with trust (Week 24)
- *Grieving the Living:* The shabar of broken expectations (Week 18)
- *Systematic Theology of Suffering:* The purpose of thlipsis (Week 28)
- *Todah:* The thanksgiving sacrifice for deliverance (Week 51)

Rest and Rhythms

- *Demamah:* Listening for the gentle whisper (Week 37)
- *Digital Sabbath:* Finding hesychia in a noisy world (Week 31)
- *Liturgy of Gratitude:* The eucharistia of the soul (Week 51)
- *Rule of Life:* Establishing a netibah of habits (Week 11)
- *Shabbat:* The holy command to cease (Week 2)
- *Shenah:* Permission to rest as a beloved child (Week 5)
- *Summer Slump:* Correcting the ekluō of spiritual apathy (Week 32)
- *Theology of the Void:* The potential of tohu wa-bohu (Week 4)

Scripture Index (NLT)

Old Testament

- Genesis 1:2 (Week 4)
- Genesis 2:2-3 (Week 2)
- Genesis 16:13 (Week 19)
- Deuteronomy 6:6-7 (Week 25)
- 1 Samuel 7:12 (Week 13)
- 1 Kings 3:7-9 (Week 41)
- 1 Kings 8:57-58 (Week 43)
- 1 Kings 19:12 (Week 37)
- Daniel 7:9 (Week 27)
- Psalm 16:5-6 (Week 16)
- Psalm 27:10 (Week 17)
- Psalm 34:18-19 (Week 18)
- Psalm 62:5 (Week 21)
- Psalm 90:12 (Week 8)
- Psalm 92:1-2 (Week 42)
- Psalm 92:14-15 (Week 45)
- Psalm 107:1-2 (Week 51)
- Psalm 127:2 (Week 5)
- Psalm 143:8 (Week 40)
- Proverbs 3:5-6 (Week 35)
- Proverbs 16:31 (Week 12)
- Proverbs 31:25-26 (Week 48)
- Isaiah 40:29-31 (Week 22)
- Jeremiah 6:16 (Week 11)
- Lamentations 3:22-23 (Week 26)

New Testament

- Matthew 5:37 (Week 23)
- Matthew 6:25-26 (Week 24)
- Matthew 6:31-33 (Week 7)
- Matthew 11:28-29 (Week 1)
- Mark 6:31 (Week 31)
- Luke 10:38-42 (Week 14)
- Romans 12:2 (Week 10)
- Romans 12:11-12 (Week 47)
- 1 Corinthians 4:17-18 (Week 28)
- 2 Corinthians 5:1-2 (Week 34)
- 2 Corinthians 12:9 (Week 15)
- Galatians 6:9 (Week 32)
- Ephesians 2:8-10 (Week 9)
- Ephesians 4:23 (Week 29)
- Philippians 2:5-7 (Week 6)
- Philippians 2:13-15 (Week 49)
- Philippians 4:3 (Week 20)
- Philippians 4:8 (Week 39)
- Hebrews 12:27-28 (Week 30)
- James 1:4 (Week 46)
- James 1:5 (Week 33)
- 2 Timothy 1:7 (Week 38)
- 2 Timothy 1:14 (Week 36)
- 2 Timothy 4:7-8 (Week 52)
- Titus 2:3 4 (Week 44)
- 1 John 3:1 (Week 3)
- Revelation 21:5 (Week 50)

www.ingramcontent.com/pod-product-compliance
Lightning Source LLC
Chambersburg PA
CBHW051509050726
47594CB00010B/4033